Auntie D's Recipes

Danielle Ackley-McPhail

Pennsville, NJ

Dedication

To all of those who indulge my need to feed.

PUBLISHED BY
Paper Phoenix Press
A division of eSpec Books
PO Box 242
Pennsville, NJ 08070
www.especbooks.com

Copyright © 2024 Danielle Ackley-McPhail

ISBN: 978-1-956463-61-3
ISBN (ebook): 978-1-956463-60-6

All rights reserved. No part of the contents of this book may be reproduced or transmitted in any form or by any means without the written permission of the publisher.

Interior and Cover Design: Danielle McPhail, McP Digital Graphics
Cover Adjustment: Mike McPhail, McP Digital Graphics
Copyediting: Greg Schauer
Photographs © Danielle McPhailpg

Contents

Let's Get Cooking! 1

Begin with Breakfast 3
Lemon Blueberry Buttermilk Pancakes 4
Taco Bake 6
Fluffy Cheese Omelet 8
Sausage Gravy 9
Cheese Blintzes 11

Bready Basics 13
Uncle Mike's Pizza Dough 14
Uncle Mike's Pretzel Dough 15
Garlic Pita Bread 18
Cheesy Biscuits 20

Let's Take a Dip 22
Basil Ricotta Cheese 23
Eggplant Caponata 24
Humus 25
Tzatziki 26
Pico De Gallo 27
Traditional Fresh Salsa 28
Fruity Peach Mango Salsa 28
Guacamole 30

Sounds Appetizing 31
Asian-Style Pot Stickers 32
Vegetarian Spring Rolls 34
Mediterranean Pita Rounds 36
Micro Taco Bowls 36
Homemade Pizza 37
Stromboli 39
Pretzel Stromboli 41
Pretzel Dogs 43
Sausage-Stuffed Mushrooms 44
Balsamic Marinated Mushrooms Kabob 45

Getting Saucy 46
Basic Gravy 47
Smoky Meatloaf Glaze 47
Meaty Spaghetti Sauce 48
Throw-Together Sauce 49

It's Soup Weather 50
Sausage Soup 51
Lentil and Ham Soup 52
Potato Leek Soup with Bacon and Cheese . . 53
Potato Celery Soup
    with Sausage and Cheese 55
Pot Roast Soup 57

That's a Crock 58
Basic Beef Stew 59
Apricot-Drenched
    Country-Style Pork Ribs 60
SauerApple Pork 61
Chili – Two Ways 62
Decadent Pot Roast 64
Root Beer Pulled Pork 65
Easy Chicken and Dumplings 66

Sides Hustle 68
Quick Sauerkraut 69
Creamy Coleslaw 70
White Bean Ragout 71
Asian Pickled Cabbage 72
Uncle Mike's Sticky White Rice 74
Uncle Mike's Mashed Potatoes 75

The Main Event 76
Fresh Salsa and Chicken Over Rice 77
Heart-Stopping,
    Tummy-Lovin' Mac and Cheese 78
Garlic-Studded,
    Rosemary-Crusted Prime Rib 81
Chicken with Lemon Garlic Rice 83
Sheppard's Pie 84
Traditional Cottage Pie 85
Seared Savory Beef over Rice 87
Vegetarian Pad Thai 88
Cheese and Onion Pierogi 89
Meat and Veg Loaf 92
Bacon-Wrapped Pork Tenderloin 93

Aren't You Sweet! 94
Spicy Applesauce 95
Caramel Pecans 96
Candied Ginger 97
Homemade Granola 100
Maple Ginger Candied Bacon 102
Bread Pudding 104
Creamy Rice Pudding 105
White Frosting 106
Auntie D's Famous Carrot Cake 107
Dark and Fudgy Chocolate Cake 108
Berry Sauce 109

Auntie D's Recipes

COOKIES! 110
Pina Colada Cookies 111
Limoncello Coconut
   with Candied Ginger Cookies 112
Rum Raisin Cookies 113
Golden Oatmeal Raisin Cookies 114
Ginger-Glazed Shortbread 115
Caramel Pecan Snickerdoodles 117
Ginger-Coconut Macaroons 118
Orange-Ginger Florentines 119
Ginger KICK! Spice Cookies 121
Lemon Ricotta Cookies 122

A BIT OF TIPPLE 123
Homemade Ginger Ale 124
Apple Bourbon Cocktail
   with Ginger Syrup 125
Just Peachy Apple Cider 125
Rum Kick 126
Shandygaff 126

ABOUT THE AUTHOR 127
OUR DISCERNING CONNOISSEURS 128

Let's Get Cooking!

I first attempted to cook when I was about five.

It was a disaster.

I'm not sure how or why I was able to get as far as I did without anyone stepping in, but my mother owned an electric frying pan and one night, I decided to make myself a grilled cheese sandwich. Just slapped cheese between the bread and dropped it in the pan.

It burned.

To this day, I cannot stand char on my food unless it is a toasted marshmallow.

It would be about fourteen years before I attempted to cook on my own again, beyond putting something in a microwave. Baking mostly, with better, if indifferent, results, followed by my famous homemade stromboli. It wasn't until I met Ruth Freedman that I took a more serious interest in cooking. She was a culinary instructor in the midst of dying from lupus, and for a brief time, I lived with her family before going off to college. The seed of my passion for cooking was planted by Ruth, who taught me by calling out directions from her bed. I still wasn't very good at it, but that is when it took root.

I bought my first cookbook from the college bookstore and started to muddle through making meals on my own. I still own that cookbook.

When I got married, I moved to New York and learned what it was to appreciate finer dining, without the budget to indulge as often as I would like. That meant learning to cook those fancy dishes for myself. Thank goodness for the Food Network and all of those chefs and shows sharing their techniques.

I have always enjoyed sharing my efforts... even before I was very good at it. My husband, Mike, bore the brunt of my learning and thirty-two years later, he has not only survived, but thrived. I honed my skills at home, but as we became authors, and then publishers, I began to share my culinary efforts with the world. Well, our world, anyway. Private parties with family, friends, and authors, launch parties celebrating our new releases at science fiction conventions. And even in the dealer's room, where convention goers could partake of my homemade flavor-infused candied ginger products.

2 Auntie D's Recipes

As my passion for cooking kindled, then blazed, I shared photos and recipes on social media, and experimented with the menus at my events. When mostly convention goers survive on the chips and cheese and other nibbles to be had at room parties, we prided ourselves on serving meal-level food. Our events have become, if I might be excused a bit of hubris, quite popular. Even legendary.

How legendary, you ask? Enough that at the time I wrote this, I was in the Quarter Finals of the Favorite Chef competition, having survived elimination in a contest that started out with around 93,000 professional and home chefs.

Sad to say, I didn't make it past the Quarter Finals, but I am grateful for the love and support shown to me and this book is one of the ways I am giving back to those who rallied behind me in that competition. For years, I have been asked for my recipes. I've generally shared specific ones at the time of asking, but those were the original source recipes without the adaptations that made them my own. I've been meaning to change that before my special touch on those recipes is lost. I have been procrastinating bringing them all together. Time to get down to it!

It is important to note that this is not a comprehensive cookbook covering all the basics and meals for any and all occasions. It is a collection of recipes I have become known for and reflect my tastes and preferences, for you to use as a supplement to your existing cookbook library.

With that in mind, I hope you enjoy Auntie D's Recipes.

Danielle Ackley-McPhail

Begin with Breakfast

Lemon Blueberry Buttermilk Pancakes
Taco Bake
Fluffy Cheese Omelet
Sausage Gravy
Cheese Blintzes

Lemon Blueberry Buttermilk Pancakes

INGREDIENTS
2½ cups all-purpose flour
3 tablespoons sugar
The zest of one lemon (optional)
2 teaspoons kosher salt
1 teaspoon baking powder
1 teaspoon baking soda
2½ cups buttermilk
8 tablespoons unsalted butter, melted
2 eggs, whites and yolks separated
1 tablespoon butter, plus more for serving
Blueberries (optional)
Powdered sugar (optional)
Maple syrup, for serving

MATERIALS
Griddle, frying pan, or cast-iron skillet
Large bowl
Microwave-safe 4-cup measuring cup
Whisk
Silicone spatula
Measuring cups and spoons
Micro-plane or zester
Two small bowls

PREPARATION

In a large bowl, add the flour, sugar, lemon zest, salt, baking powder, and baking soda and whisk to combine. Set aside until you are ready, then separate your eggs, placing the whites and yolks into separate bowls.

Cut your butter into chunks and place them in the measuring cup. In fifteen second intervals, melt the butter in the microwave. Add the buttermilk, egg yolks, and vanilla, then whisk to combine.

Carefully add the buttermilk mixture to the dry ingredients and gently fold with a silicone spatula until just combined. It is okay if you see some dry flour. Do not overmix it or your pancakes will be flat and heavy.

Whisk the egg whites and fold them in until just combined. Again, do not overmix. Some lumps are okay.

Let the batter rest for 15–30 minutes at room temperature.

Add the butter to the griddle and heat over medium low heat. Once the butter has melted and is bubbling, reduce the heat to medium-low and add 1/4 cup of batter to the pan.

Cook for 2–3 minutes, until bubbles start to appear on the surface. If adding any toppings like chocolate chips or blueberries, and you haven't just folded them into the batter, sprinkle them over the pancake now. Flip the pancake over and cook for another 1–2 minutes, until golden brown. Repeat with the remaining batter.

Serve the pancakes with butter and maple syrup.

While my recipe is for Lemon Blueberry pancakes, you can, of course, just make plain buttermilk pancakes or add your own combination of additions, though take care with anything wet that will affect the batter.

My goal, when cooking, is to enjoy. That doesn't always mesh with eating healthy. When I make these pancakes, I use a two-burner griddle and make a pound of bacon first. I leave the grease in the griddle, seasoning it with the drippings before running butter across the hot surface and adding the batter for each round of pancakes.

My niece, who is a nurse practitioner, was horrified. But darn if those pancakes didn't have a nice, crispy edge and taste amazing. There wasn't a pancake left.

Taco Bake

INGREDIENTS
1 pound of ground beef, browned and seasoned with taco seasoning
1 cup of taco toppings of your choice (I use chopped up tomatoes, black olives, and scallions, and sometimes frozen corn)
1 cup of shredded cheddar
1 batch of cheesy biscuits, uncooked (pg. 20)

MATERIALS
Casserole dish (9 x 9 inches, or of a size suitable for the volume of contents.)
Non-stick spray

PREPARATION
Preheat oven to 450F.

In a greased casserole dish layer, add the taco meat and toppings evenly, then spread the cheese over that. Last, take the raw biscuits and place them on top, being sure to leave space for the biscuits to expand, about half an inch between each one. Do not place them too closely together or the heat will not distribute evenly and some of the biscuits might end up undercooked.

Bake in the preheated oven for approximately 25 minutes.

When I make this, it is generally with leftovers from taco night, but there is nothing saying you can't just decide to make it fresh.

For the biscuits, since this is a taco bake, I add both taco seasoning and shredded cheddar to the dough. Not too much, but enough to give it a little added flavor. Also, a full batch of biscuit dough is likely too much for this recipe, particularly if you are working with leftovers, so either halve the biscuit recipe or just use the extra dough to make individual biscuits when you are done.

Fluffy Cheesy Omelet

INGREDIENTS
5 eggs
½ cup milk
½ cup of desired additives, diced
½ cup of shredded cheese
Seasonings to taste

MATERIALS
10-inch skillet with a lid
Tall container (I use a large deli container or a smoothie shaker)
Fork
Non-stick spray

PREPARATION
Combine the eggs, milk, and seasonings in the tall container. With your fork, whisk until thoroughly combined and you have introduced a lot of air into the mixture. Spray your pan and preheat over medium heat. Once it is hot, pour in the egg mixture and quickly add in the desired additives (or not) and the cheese. Reduce the heat to medium low and cover, occasionally swirling the pan to spread the still-liquid egg more evenly across the surface. While the heat is cooking from below, the steam will cook the egg on the surface, creating a thick, fluffy omelet. As soon as the moisture on the surface dries/firms up, remove the pan from the heat and slide the omelet onto a plate. Serves two.

NOTE: this method will produce color on the bottom. As long as your heat isn't too high, it shouldn't be too dark. Don't worry, color is flavor.

Sausage Gravy

INGREDIENTS
1 package pre-cooked breakfast sausage crumbles, or half a tube of breakfast sausage, browned into crumbles
¼ cup flour
2½ cups milk
salt and freshly ground black pepper to taste

MATERIALS
Sauté pan
Silicon spatula
Measuring cups (dry and wet)

PREPARATION
Cook the sausage in a large skillet over medium heat until thoroughly heated and/or cooked through, stirring frequently.

Stir in the flour until well combined and you cannot see any white left. Gradually add milk, stirring continuously, until the gravy thickens and comes to a boil. Reduce heat to medium-low; simmer and stir for two more minutes. Season to taste with salt and pepper. Go too light on this, and the gravy will just taste like milk and flour paste; go too heavy, and the salt or pepper overwhelms. My advice is to add a little seasoning and taste before adding more.

Serve over sourdough toast or the cheesy biscuits from page 20.

Cheese Blintzes

INGREDIENTS

Crepe Batter:
1 cup milk
1 cup all-purpose flour
¼ cup cold water
3 large eggs
2 tablespoons vegetable oil
1 tablespoon white sugar
½ teaspoon salt
¼ teaspoon vanilla extract
1 tablespoon butter, or as needed

Cheese Filling:
1 ½ cups farmer's or ricotta cheese (pg. 23)
½ cup cream cheese, at room temperature
1 large egg
3 tablespoons powdered sugar, divided, or more as needed
The zest from one medium lemon
1 pinch of salt

MATERIALS

Four-cup measuring cup
Medium bowl
Silicon spatula
cooking spray
Flipper
Measuring spoons and cups
Baking dish
10-inch skillet

PREPARATION

Make the batter: Combine milk, flour, water, eggs, oil, sugar, salt, and vanilla in a blender (I just whisk all of this directly in the measuring cup). Blend until completely smooth, 1 or 2 minutes, scraping down the sides as needed. Let batter sit at room temperature for 30 minutes.

While the batter is sitting, whisk the ricotta cheese, cream cheese, egg, 2 tablespoons powdered sugar, lemon zest, and salt together in a mixing bowl until thoroughly combined. Cover and refrigerate until needed.

When batter has rested, pour a measure of batter into a ¼ cup measuring cup. Then heat a 10-inch, nonstick skillet over medium-high heat. You will need to spray the pan in between each crepe. Take the pan off of the heat, spray it, then, when it is still off the heat, pour the batter and swirl the pan to spread the batter until it coats the bottom of the skillet as best as you can in a full circle before placing the pan back on the heat, otherwise the batter starts to cook too quick for you to swirl it easily.

Cook until the surface looks dry, about 1 minute, then with your flipper, turn the crêpe and briefly cook the other side, about 30 seconds. Slide the finished crepe onto a plate and repeat until there is no batter left.

Preheat the oven to 325 F. Lightly grease a baking dish.

Spoon 3 to 4 tablespoons filling onto each crêpe, about 1 inch from the edge nearest you. Fold the edge over the filling and flatten slightly.

Fold in both sides, then roll the crêpe into a small, filled rectangle (blintz), ending with the seam on the bottom.

Melt butter in a large skillet over medium heat. Working in batches, cook several blintzes at a time until golden brown, turning gently, about 1 minute per side. Transfer to the baking dish.

Bake about 12 minutes in the preheated oven to firm up the filling.

Cool blintzes for 10 minutes before serving.

Serve topped with powdered sugar and fresh berries, or with Berry Sauce (pg. 109) and/or fresh berries and whipped cream.

BREADY BASICS

**Uncle Mike's Pizza Dough
Uncle Mike's Pretzel Dough
Garlic Pita Bread
Cheesy Biscuits**

Uncle Mike's Pizza Dough

INGREDIENTS
1 .25-ounce package of active dry yeast, or 2 ½ teaspoons
1 teaspoon of white sugar
1 cup of warm water (110F)
2½ cups flour (bread or all-purpose)
2 tablespoons olive oil
1 teaspoon salt
1 teaspoon garlic powder
2 teaspoons fresh rosemary chopped (or to taste - optional)

MATERIALS
Medium bowl
Large bowl
Measuring spoons
Plastic wrap

PREPARATION

In a medium bowl, dissolve yeast and sugar in warm water. Let stand until creamy, about ten minutes.

Stir in flour, salt, rosemary, garlic, and half the oil. Beat into a ball.

Grease the large bowl with the remaining oil and transfer the dough ball to that bowl, rolling it around to coat with oil.

Cover the dough with plastic wrap and tuck down the sides. Place a towel or plate over the bowl and keep bowl in a warm place. Should rise in an hour or two.

I use this in both my Stromboli and Flatbread Pizza recipes.

Uncle Mike's Pretzel Dough

INGREDIENTS
12 fluid ounces of water
1 tablespoon white sugar
2 teaspoons kosher salt
1 .25-ounce package of active dry yeast, or 2 ½ teaspoons
4 ½ cups bread flour
¼ cup unsalted butter, melted
2 large egg yolks, or more as needed
2 tablespoons water
10 cups water
¼ cup baking soda

Topping suggestions (all as needed)
Kosher salt
Oregano
Parmesan Cheese
Sesame Seeds

MATERIALS
Bread maker or stand mixer or large bowl
Measuring cups
Measuring spoons
Rolling pin
Pastry knife/board scrapper/pizza cutter
Large pot
Kitchen spider
Baking sheets
Parchment paper
Cooking spray
Timer

PREPARATION
Preheat the oven to 450F.

Line two baking sheets with parchment paper or grease with vegetable oil. Set aside until needed. (If your pans are thin, you can double them up or use silicon sheets to prevent the bottom of your pretzels from getting overbaked.)

Heat the water or beer in a saucepan over low heat or microwave for 15 seconds until it reaches 110F.

16 Auntie D's Recipes

Combine the warm water, sugar, and 2 teaspoons kosher salt in a bowl or stand mixer. Sprinkle the yeast on top and let stand for 5 minutes until the yeast softens and begins to form a creamy foam. (If using instant yeast, you can add all ingredients directly to your mixing bowl or machine. You only need to proof the yeast if you use active dry yeast.) If you want to experiment with a flavored dough, try adding garlic powder, onion powder, minced rosemary, cinnamon, or other spice combinations to the dough at this stage.

By hand or using the dough hook attachment from your stand mixer, mix the ingredients together until they form a soft, supple dough. Knead by hand or in your stand mixer for either ten or five minutes, depending on your method. Lightly grease your bowl and place your dough ball inside. Cover and let proof for about one hour and fifteen minutes, until doubled.

If using a bread machine, place the bread flour and butter in the bread machine, add the yeast mixture, then select the dough cycle.

While the dough is proofing, stir baking soda into 10 cups water in a large pot until dissolved, and bring to a boil. Then beat the egg yolks in a small bowl with 1 tablespoon water; set aside until needed. You may need more egg yolk than specified.

After the dough has proofed, turn it out onto a lightly-oiled surface and punch out the air.

Once the dough is wrapped or shaped as you desire—or in batches, if you choose—drop 2 or 3 pretzels into the boiling water at a time for 30 seconds then using the spider, move them to the baking sheets. Arrange the boiled pretzel items on the prepared baking sheets with room to expand. Brush each with the egg yolk mixture, and sprinkle with the remaining 1/4 cup salt or preferred topping.

Bake in the preheated oven until golden brown, about 15 minutes.

Want to do something fun? Take Nutella, or peanut butter (creamy and not natural-style), and freeze small scoops of each, keeping them in the freezer until you are ready to make your pretzel bites. When your dough is ready, cut off a nugget-sized piece and roll it flat, but not too thin. Place one of your frozen treats in the middle and wrap the dough around it, being sure to press together any edges really well to seal them. Keep your finished nuggets in the refrigerator until you are ready to boil.

You can also make pretzel buns by shaping the dough the way you would a roll and scoring the top and preparing them per the standard instructions. These are great for breakfast sandwiches or hamburgers, especially if you grill the buns before using them.

Garlic Pita Bread

INGREDIENTS
1 .25-ounce package of active dry yeast, or 2 ½ teaspoons
1 cup warm water, 110F
1 cup all-purpose flour
1 ½ tablespoons olive oil
1 ¾ teaspoons salt
Granulated garlic, to taste
1 ¾ cups all-purpose flour, or more as needed
1 teaspoon olive oil, divided

MATERIALS
Large bowl or stand mixer
Measuring spoons and cups
Knife
Rolling pin
Plastic wrap
Griddle or skillet

PREPARATION

Place yeast in the bowl of a stand mixer and add 1 cup warm water and 1 cup flour. Whisk together, then let sit until mixture bubbles and foams, 15 to 20 minutes.

Add 1½ tablespoons olive oil and salt into the yeast mixture, followed by 1¾ cups flour. Mix at low speed, using a dough hook attachment, until dough is soft, supple, and slightly sticky. If dough sticks to the sides of the bowl, add up to ¼ cup more flour, a little at a time.

Knead dough with machine on low speed until slightly springy and still soft, 5 to 6 minutes. Turn dough out onto a floured work surface and form into a ball.

Wipe inside of bowl with ¼ teaspoon olive oil. Turn dough around in bowl to coat; cover bowl with foil and let sit until dough has doubled in size, about 2 hours.

Remove dough from bowl and place onto a floured work surface. Lightly pat into a flat shape about 1-inch thick. Use a knife to cut dough into 8 equal pieces.

Form each piece into a small round ball with a smooth top, pulling dough from the sides and tucking the ends underneath the bottom.

Cover dough balls with lightly oiled plastic wrap and let rest for 30 minutes.

Transfer the dough balls to a lightly floured work surface and sprinkle the tops with flour. One at a time, gently pat the dough with your fingers, forming a flat, round bread about ¼-inch thick. Let the shaped dough rest for 5 minutes

Brush a griddle or cast-iron skillet with the remaining ¾ teaspoon olive oil and place over medium-high heat. Lay dough into the hot skillet; cook until puffy and the bottom has brown spots and blisters, about 3 minutes. Flip, cook 2 more minutes, and flip back onto original side to cook for about 30 more seconds. Pita bread will begin to puff up and fill with hot air. Stack cooked breads on a plate; when cool enough to handle, slice breads in half and open the pocket inside for stuffing.

Cheesy Biscuits

INGREDIENTS
2 cups all-purpose flour
1 tablespoon baking powder
½ teaspoon salt
1 stick frozen butter
½ cup freshly grated cheese of your choice
¾ cup cold milk
Extra flour as needed

MATERIALS
Large grate micro-plane or box grater
Bowl
Rolling pin
Cookie cutter or bench scraper
Baking tray
Parchment paper, foil, or silicon mat

PREPARATION

Gather all ingredients and preheat oven to 450F.

In a large mixing bowl sift together flour, baking powder, and salt. Grate in the butter and add the cheese.

Pour milk into your flour mixture and combine with a fork. Mix in milk until dough is soft, moist and pulls away from the side of the bowl. Once it is well combined, turn the dough out onto a lightly floured surface and knead the dough briefly, 5 to 7 times.

Roll the dough out into a ½-inch-thick sheet and cut out biscuits with a floured cookie cutter. Press together unused dough and repeat the rolling and cutting procedure. If you want to cut down on how much the dough is worked, instead of using a cookie cutter, you can use a bench scraper to cut the rolled-out dough into biscuit squares.

Place biscuits on ungreased baking sheets and bake in preheated oven until golden brown, about 10 minutes.

SUGGESTIONS
These are great served with sausage gravy or used as a topper for a taco-bake. I have also used them to make pigs in a blanket that are simply divine!

When I need to add butter to a recipe where the intention is to create something flaky or crumbly, like a crumb crust on a pie, I use frozen butter and grate it into the mixture. Before I grate it, I roll the stick of butter in the flour in the bowl to keeping it from melting on my fingers or the grater. Periodically, I will repeat this process, turning the stick so that the portion that has softened is grated away. This sounds involved, but it is a fairly quick process and ensures the butter is more evenly distributed in the mixture, without getting too soft from overworking.

Let's Take a Dip

Basil Ricotta Cheese
Eggplant Caponata
Humus
Tzatziki
Traditional Fresh Salsa
Fruity Peach Mango Salsa
Pico De Gallo
Guacamole

Basil Ricotta Cheese

INGREDIENTS
4 cups whole milk
½ cup heavy cream
1¼ teaspoon kosher salt
5 basil leaves on the stem
Granulated garlic to taste
2 tablespoons white vinegar

MATERIALS
Saucepan
Strainer
Bowl
Cheese cloth
Silicon spatula
Candy thermometer
Measuring spoons and cups
Timer

PREPARATION
Place a fine strainer or colander in a medium-sized bowl and line with cheesecloth.

Combine milk, cream, salt, garlic, and basil in a heavy-bottomed saucepan. Heat on medium-high to 195F, stirring occasionally in a figure-8 pattern. When the mixture reaches temperature remove the pot from the heat. Remove and discard the basil leaves and add the vinegar. Stir in a figure-8 again for about six seconds, then let the mixture sit for six minutes.

Once the curds have formed, carefully pour the mixture into the cheesecloth-lined strainer. Let it drain for between 20 and 45 minutes depending on how firm/dry you want your cheese, then lift it out of the strainer in the cheesecloth, settle it in a bowl and fold the cheesecloth over the top. Let it come to room temperature, then refrigerate.

> **This can be used as a spread, filling, or component in another recipe. If you are using the ricotta for a pastry or sweet application, omit the basil leaves and garlic, and substitute vanilla or the flavoring of your choice, such as a cinnamon stick or spices, herbs, or teas in a satchel (remove as above, before you add the vinegar.) Or, if you prefer a simpler ricotta, omit the basil and garlic or any other flavoring.**

Eggplant Caponata

INGREDIENTS

1 pound of eggplants cut into 1 ½ inch cubes
¼ cup olive oil
1 yellow onion, diced
4 cloves garlic, grated
1 can diced tomatoes 15 ounce
1 red bell pepper diced
½ cup green and black olives chopped
¼ cup capers
1 tsp salt
¼ teaspoon black pepper

MATERIALS

Baking Sheet
Foil
Non-stick spray
Medium bowl
Sauté pan

PREPARATION

Preheat the oven to 400F. Line a baking sheet with foil and coat with non-stick spray.

Place the eggplant into a bowl with two tablespoons of olive oil and a bit of salt. Mix to combine, then spread on the prepared pan.

Roast the eggplants in the oven for 20 minutes.

While it is roasting, heat the rest of the olive oil in a pan over medium heat.

Sauté the onion and garlic until translucent.

Add in the diced tomatoes and red bell peppers and cook for about 10 minutes.

Add in roasted eggplant, chopped olives, and capers. Cook for 5 minutes.

Season with salt and pepper.

Top with parsley and serve warm with crusty bread.

Humus

INGREDIENTS
1 15-ounce can chickpeas, rinsed
3 tablespoons of lemon juice
2 teaspoons olive oil
½ cup plain low or no-fat Greek yogurt
3 cloves fresh garlic, minced or crushed
¼ teaspoon black pepper
½ teaspoon salt
1 teaspoon cumin or to taste
1 tablespoon of water

MATERIALS
High-sided bowl
Measuring spoons
Knife
Cutting board
Stick blender or food processor
Storage container with an airtight seal

PREPARATION
Combine all ingredients in a food processor (or high-sided bowl, if using stick blender), mix well until all is blended and there are no large chunks.

Store finished dip in refrigerator in airtight container.

SUGGESTIONS
Use as a dip with pita bread, chips, or veggies of your choice

Very nice on whole grain bread with purple grapes (halved) or kalamata olives.

Use lightly in place of mayo or other condiments on sandwiches or as the main protein in the sandwich paired with roasted red pepper, feta cheese, cucumbers or basil.

VARIATIONS
In place of chickpeas try using edamame (soybeans) or black beans

Try adding kalamata olives and feta cheese for a richer flavor

Omit water and instead include roasted red pepper in base recipe

Tzatziki

INGREDIENTS
1 cup plain low or no-fat Greek yogurt
2 English cucumbers peeled (if you use regular cucumbers you will need to deseed)
The juice of half a lemon
2 teaspoons olive oil
1 clove fresh garlic, minced or crushed
Salt and black pepper (to taste)
1 tablespoon fresh dill, chopped (or to taste)
1 tablespoon fresh mint, chopped (or to taste)

MATERIALS
Cheese cloth
Box grater
High-sided bowl
Measuring spoons
Knife
Cutting board
Storage container with an airtight seal

PREPARATION
Using a plate or a bowl, cover it with your cheese cloth. Then take your box grater and grate your cucumber over the cheese cloth using the large grate. Once your cucumber is grated, gather the edges of the cheese cloth up into your hand so you have a pouch containing the cucumber. Twist the ends as tight as you are able to squeeze out as much moisture as you can, occasionally squeezing the mass directly until the cucumber is as dry as you can make it.

Combined the strained cucumber and the other ingredients into a bowl and mix thoroughly.

Store finished dip in refrigerator in airtight container.

SUGGESTIONS
Use as a dip with pita bread, chips, or veggies of your choice
Use lightly in place of mayo or other condiments on sandwiches

Pico De Gallo

INGREDIENTS
3 large tomatoes, deseeded and diced
¼ cup cilantro, roughly chopped
¼ cup finely chopped white or purple onion
1½ tablespoon finely chopped Jalapeño, or to taste
1 to 2 tablespoons lime juice, or to taste
¾ tsp kosher salt

MATERIALS
Knife
Cutting board
Bowl
Food-grade gloves

PREPARATION
Combine the ingredients in a bowl and mix well. Set aside for 5 to 20 minutes for the flavors to blend.

This can be made up to a day in advance. If you are making this ahead of time, do not add the lime or salt until you are ready to serve, or the mixture will be too wet. When you are ready to serve, drain the excess liquid from the tomatoes and add the lime juice and salt just before serving.

Traditional Fresh Salsa

INGREDIENTS
1 large or two medium ripe tomatoes
1 medium onion (of preferred type)
1 finely chopped Jalapeño, or to taste
1 cup chopped bell pepper (green, red, or mixed colors, to taste)
2 cloves chopped garlic
2 tablespoons of fresh chopped cilantro
1 tablespoon Lime juice
¼ teaspoon salt
¼ teaspoon black pepper

MATERIALS
Large high-sided bowl
Small bowl
Measuring spoons
Knife
Mixing spoon
Cutting board
Stick blender or food processor
Storage container with an airtight seal
Food-grade gloves

PREPARATION
Rough chop all produce ingredients and combine into large bowl, mix well. Take roughly two-thirds of the resulting mixture and set aside in a smaller bowl. On the remaining quantity use the stick blender until pureed. Return reserved vegetables to the bowl and add liquid and seasoning ingredients, stir to combine, leaving final mixture chunky. (If you like a more solid salsa omit the puree step.

VARIATIONS
Fruity Peach Mango Salsa – Substitute one large mango and a ripe peach for the tomatoes, and proceed as written.

While cutting the jalapeno, take great care not to touch your face, eyes, or other sensitive areas.

If possible, wear food-service, latex or nitril gloves while cutting them. If those are not available, I have used plastic sandwich bags to keep the juice from coming into contact with my skin.

This was a painful lesson to learn as the compound that gives chilis their heat can remain on your skin even after washing, which can be very painful later if you touch any of the above.

Once you are done cutting, if you are wearing gloves, rinse your board and utensils thoroughly, then pull the gloves off so that they are inside out directly into the garbage, so you don't come in contact with the contaminated surface. If you are not wearing gloves, be sure to wash your board, utensils, and hands very thoroughly with soap and water several times to minimize the potential of spreading the heat compound through casual touch.

My method of cutting jalapeno is to cut them in half, scrape out the ribs and seeds, and to cut the chili into very thin strips, then finely dice those strips so that the heat is well distributed throughout whatever I plan to add the chili to.

Guacamole

INGREDIENTS
Three ripe avocados
The juice of one lime
Two plum tomatoes, deseeded and diced
1 tsp kosher salt
1 clove garlic, grated
1 finely chopped Jalapeño, or to taste
¼ cup sour cream

MATERIALS
Knife
Cutting board
Bowl
Potato masher
Measuring cups and spoons
Food-grade gloves

PREPARATION
Cut the avocados in half and remove the pits. Using a large spoon, scoop out the flesh of the avocado into the bowl. Using your potato masher, a fork, or a food processor, mash the flesh until it is the desired consistency, then combine all of the ingredients into the bowl and mix well.

I know, sour cream is not a traditional ingredient, but I assure you that it both helps make a creamy guac and minimizes the tendency for the guac to oxidize into that hideous brown-green color.

Sounds Appetizing

Asian-Style Pot Stickers
Vegetarian Spring Rolls
Mediterranean Pita Rounds
Micro Taco Bowls
Homemade Pizza
Stromboli
Pretzel Stromboli
Pretzel Dogs
Sausage-Stuffed Mushrooms

Balsamic Marinated
Mushrooms Kabob

Asian-Style Pot Stickers

INGREDIENTS
1 package of wonton wrappers, or as needed
1¾ pound ground meat of your choice
1 tablespoon fresh ginger, minced
4 cloves garlic, minced
3 tablespoons sesame oil
4 tablespoons soy sauce
2 green onions sliced thin
5 cups Chinese cabbage, chopped fine

MATERIALS
Electric frying pan with lid or steamer
Bowl with air-tight lid
Measuring spoons and cups
Large platter
Small plate
Conventional teaspoon
Several quart-sized freezer ziplock bags

PREPARATION
Mix all the ingredients in a large bowl except for the wrappers, keep those on a plate covered by a damp towel. Lay one wrapper on the small plate and place one round teaspoon of mixture in the middle. Wet the edges of the wonton wrapper with water and fold the wrapper over into a triangle, firmly press the edges together and then shape into a half circle. Repeat. (I have taken to shaping these into purses, rather than triangles, by bringing up all four points to the center over the mixture and then pressing the edges together for a complete seal. The purses are easier to manage in the frying pan.)

If you intend to steam the dumplings arrange them in your steamer and steam them for 10 to 15 minutes. If you intend to fry them, put two tablespoons of olive oil in a frying pan on medium heat. Fry for two minutes until the bottoms are golden brown, then pour ½ cup of water into the pan and cover with lid. Let them steam for about 7 minutes. The mix is likely enough to make nearly 100 dumplings, which is fine if you want them for a party, but if you just want them for a meal make the quantity you need (probably 4 to 6 per person) and freeze the balance of the mixture in one-meal portions using the freezer ziplock bags. Do not prep out the pot stickers until you intend to cook them as the wrappers absorb moisture and tend to stick together. If you are making this for a meal, rather than an appetizer, it serves well with edamame and white rice.

VARIATIONS
For Chicken and Lemongrass Pot Stickers use ground chicken, replace green onions with diced lemongrass (found in the produce section among the fresh herbs), and replace the Chinese cabbage with finely diced celery and carrots.

For Double-Pork Pot Stickers use ½ ground pork and ½ loose sweet Italian sausage.

Vegetarian Spring Rolls

INGREDIENTS
6 Rice wrappers
1 small cucumber or three inches of an English cucumber, deseeded and cut thin in 2-inch slices
1 Bell Pepper, sliced thin lengthwise
1 green onion, sliced thin in 2-inch ribbons
½ cup Asian Pickled Cabbage (pg. 72)
1 teaspoon each soy sauce and hoisin sauce
2 teaspoons sesame oil
Pepper

MATERIALS
Cutting board
Knife
Tray
Frying pan
Small bowl
Deep plate or shallow bowl the size of the rice wrappers
Dinner plate

PREPARATION
Put one teaspoon each of sesame oil, soy sauce, and hoisin sauce into a small bowl and season with black pepper. Add your cucumber and scallions to the bowl and stir until everything is evenly coated and set aside.

Heat a teaspoon of sesame oil in a fry pan and sprinkle with black pepper. Add the bell pepper slices and sauté until half-cooked.

Take your pepper slices, your cucumber/scallion mixture, and the Asian pickled cabbage and make six even piles on your cutting board. Spoon any remaining sauce evenly among the piles.

Fill your deep plate with about half an inch of warm water. Take one rice wrapper and soak it in the water until it is no longer stiff. Carefully lift it out of the water by the edges and lay it flat on the dinner plate. Blot the surface with a paper towel to remove any excess water.

Take one of your piles of vegetables and place it one inch from the bottom of your wrapper, centered. Fold the bottom over the vegetables and then fold over the sides about the same measure. Tucking the vegetables tight as you go, roll the wrapper until it forms a shape similar to an egg roll. Place the finished roll on the tray, leaving room for the other five rolls without them touching. Repeat until all your vegetables have been used.

Mediterranean Pita Rounds

INGREDIENTS
1 bag of pita chips
1 cup of Humus (pg. 25)
8 ounce of finely crumbled feta cheese
1 jar of kalamata olives and/or roasted red pepper

MATERIALS
Serving platter
Cutting board
Conventional teaspoon

PREPARATION
Lay whole pita chips flat on serving platter. Place a dollop of humus mixture in the center of chip and swirl to coat, sprinkle with a few crumbles of feta cheese and top with either ½ of a kalamata olive or a teaspoon of diced roasted red pepper.

Micro Taco Bowls

INGREDIENTS
1 bag of scoop-style tortilla chips
½ pound ground beef
½ packet taco mix
8 ounces of shredded cheddar
8 ounces of Traditional Fresh Salsa (pg. 28)
8 ounces of sour cream, or as needed
10 black olives sliced, or as needed (optional)
1 can sliced jalapeños, or as needed (optional)

MATERIALS
Serving platter
Teaspoon
Frying pan

PREPARATION
Brown the meat, drain it, then season per the directions on the seasoning packet. Arrange tortilla chips on serving platter with the mouth of the bowl face up. Place a small amount of the seasoned beef in the bottom. Not too much. Top that with salsa, a very small dollop of sour cream and a few pieces of shredded cheese. Garnish with either a black olive slice or jalapeno slice.

HOMEMADE PIZZA

INGREDIENTS
1 ball Uncle Mike's Pizza Dough* (pg. 14)
2 cups shredded mozzarella
8 ounces of ricotta (pg. 23)
Sauce (jarred tomato or pesto sauce works best)
Oregano
Parmesan Cheese
Toppings of your choice
Flour

MATERIALS
Rolling Pin
Clean counter or rolling sheet
Pastry knife
Baking sheet (without sides preferred) or pizza stone
Aluminum foil or parchment paper
Non-stick spray (for use with foil only)
Fork
Pizza cutter

PREPARATION
If using a pizza stone, place it in the oven and pre-heat the oven to its highest temperature. If using a pan, simply pre-heat the oven to the highest temperature.

Use a pastry knife to cut the dough ball in half or quarters, set extra portions aside. Take your rolling pin and lightly flour. If dough is sticky, lightly flour that as well, but don't flour the counter or surface you are rolling out on. Roll dough out into a rough rectangle, (do not roll it too thin or it will tear during transfer). Lightly flour and drape over your rolling pin to transfer it to the cookie sheet (if this stage gives you trouble you can try rolling out the dough directly on the cookie sheet, but it takes practice and a sheet without sides, or a rolling pin that will fit within the confines of your cookie sheet if it has sides. Flatten more if needed. Once the dough is the desired size and thickness, take your fork and perforate every inch or so to prevent the dough from forming an air pocket and bubbling. Spread a thin layer of sauce or ricotta then top with the toppings of your choice. Sprinkle liberally with cheese.

Bake for about 9 minutes or until golden brown. Watch closely as individual oven temperatures may differ. You want the bottom crisp, but not burnt, and the cheese melted and slightly browned. Remove tray from oven and use a pizza cutter to slice into slices of roughly one inch by three inches if using as an appetizer, or larger slices if eating as a meal.

38 Auntie D's Recipes

If you are using this for a party you can make them in advance, cut them into appetizer slices, and freeze them in a large ziplock, then just defrost and plate when it is time for the party. Freezes well.

VARIATIONS
Toppings can be anything you would have on a pizza, including plum tomatoes, pepperoni, sausage, artichoke, roasted red pepper, olives, green pepper slices, fresh basil, fresh garlic, onions, chicken…etc, etc.

SUGGESTIONS
This is best warm out of the oven, but can also be served cold as an appetizer if you don't have a way to reheat it.

* You can also buy raw dough at a pizza place, bakery, or frozen in most supermarkets.

STROMBOLI

INGREDIENTS
1 ball Uncle Mike's Pizza Dough* (pg. 14)

TOPPING SUGGESTIONS
Kosher salt
Oregano
Parmesan Cheese
Sesame Seeds

FILLING SUGGESTIONS
pepperoni or desired lunch meat sliced very thin
browned sausage finely crumbled
broccoli florets, finely chopped
Fresh spinach
Mozzarella, cheddar, ricotta, etc, strained, finely grated, or thinly sliced

MATERIALS
Rolling Pin
Clean counter or rolling sheet
Pastry knife
Baking sheet with sides
Aluminum foil or parchment paper
Non-stick spray (for use with foil only)
Knife
Large wire cooling rack
Two large spatulas

PREPARATION
Pre-heat oven to 375F.

Use a pastry knife to cut the dough ball in half, set half aside. Take your rolling pin and lightly flour. If dough is sticky, lightly flour that as well, but don't flour the counter or surface you are rolling out on. Roll dough out into a rough rectangle, (do not roll it too thin or it will tear during rolling or blow through during baking). Once the dough is the desired size, cover with slices of pepperoni so that they overlap, leave about half an inch to an inch of the dough uncovered on all sides for folding and rolling. Sprinkle evenly with shredded cheese (don't use too much or the pressure during baking will cause the sides of your Stromboli to blow out, even with vent holes). Fold over the edge closest to you so it just overlaps the pepperoni and cheese combination, pinching the dough where it lays against the other dough surface to anchor it in place. Do the same with both sides, leaving the top as is. Slowly roll and tuck the dough into a loaf, making sure the sides stay folded over. Lightly pinch the top edge and the sides, if needed, to the rolled dough to seal the loaf. Be careful not to tear a hole in the dough as you do so. Place the loaf on baking sheet that has been covered in foil or parchment paper. Cut three vent holes in the top of the loaf, being sure to go through the pepperoni. Coat the loaf with melted butter or milk or egg yolk beaten with some water and season top with spices and a sprinkling of parmesan cheese. Repeat with remaining ingredients. You can bake two on a baking sheet but make sure there is space between the loaves so they do not stick to one another when they expand.

Bake for 26 minutes or until golden brown. Remove carefully from the baking sheet, supporting the length of the loaves with a spatula on either end. Serve hot or let cool completely before wrapping in foil for storage.

Freezes well. Multiply the above components for large batches, extra components usually freeze well.

Good with most variations of meat, cheese, or vegetables, but be cautious of using elements that add extra moisture, such as roasted red peppers.

VARIATIONS

I have made this in the following tasty combinations: Fresh Spinach and Mozzarella, Fresh Spinach and Ricotta with Mozzarella, Broccoli and Cheddar, Ricotta and Garlic with Mozzarella, Ricotta and Pepperoni with Mozzarella, Chip Steak with Provolone or Mozzarella, Ground Beef and Cheddar or Sausage and Mozzarella. The possible variations are endless.

SUGGESTIONS

This is best warm out of the oven but can be reheated or even eaten cold. If you are heating leftovers in the microwave, be sure to cut into slices of about half an inch or so wide and only microwave for about thirty seconds. If you are reheating in the oven, preheat to 350F, wrap the stromboli in foil whole and heat for about twenty minutes, then cut and serve.

For single-serving sizes you can quarter the dough instead of halving it and make a meal-sized Stromboli.

---

* You can also buy raw dough at a pizza place, bakery, or frozen in most supermarkets.

Pretzel Stromboli

INGREDIENTS
1 ball Uncle Mike's Pretzel Dough (pg. 15)
Flour (for dusting the work surface)
10 cups water
¼ cup baking soda
2 egg yolks
2 tablespoons of water

TOPPING SUGGESTIONS
Kosher salt
Oregano
Parmesan Cheese
Sesame Seeds

FILLING SUGGESTIONS
pepperoni or desired lunch meat sliced very thin
browned sausage finely crumbled
broccoli florets, finely chopped
Fresh spinach
Mozzarella, cheddar, ricotta, strained, finely grated or thinly sliced into narrow strips

MATERIALS
Rolling pin
Pastry knife/board scrapper/pizza cutter
Basting brush
Small bowl
Large pot
Kitchen spider
Baking sheets
Parchment paper
Cooking spray
Timer

PREPARATION
Pre-heat the oven to 450F.

Leave the dough in a ball, cut off pieces as needed, covering the ball in a damp towel as you work. Using a rolling pin, roll out the individual piece into a roughly four-inch-by-four-inch square. Lay down your toppings in even layers of cheese topped by even layers meat or vegetable, fold over the sides, then from one of the ends roll

42 Auntie D's Recipes

the dough over the toppings in a pinwheel, making sure to keep the sides and the filling tucked in as you roll. Once you have it rolled, press the sides and the open edge together to seal them closed.

Once everything is wrapped—or in batches, if you choose—drop 2 or 3 strombolis into the boiling water at a time for 30 seconds then using the spider, move them to the baking sheets. Arrange the boiled pretzel items on the prepared baking sheets and pierce them through to vent the steam. This will minimize the tendency for the fillings to blow out the sides. Brush each with the egg yolk mixture, and sprinkle with the remaining 1/4 cup salt or preferred topping.

Bake in the preheated oven until golden brown, about 15 minutes.

Pretzel Dogs

INGREDIENTS
1 ball of Uncle Mike's Pretzel Dough (pg. 15)
18 hot dogs, cocktail weenies, or to taste (You can always halve the recipe, make pretzels out of the extra, or freeze the unused dough)
1 pound of the cheeses of your choice, finely grated or thinly sliced into narrow strips (optional)
Flour (for dusting the work surface)
10 cups water
¼ cup baking soda
2 egg yolks
2 tablespoons water

MATERIALS
Rolling pin
Pastry knife/board scrapper/pizza cutter
Large pot
Kitchen spider
Baking sheets
Parchment paper
Cooking spray
Timer

PREPARATION
Pre-heat the oven to 450F.

Roll pretzel dough into a 10 x 20-inch rectangle and cut it into 18 1-inch-wide strips, then wrap each strip tightly around a hot dog in a spiral, pinching the edges to seal, and leaving the ends open. About half an inch of hot dog should peek out of each end of the dough wrapper. If desired, you can wrap the dogs in cheese before wrapping them in dough. Another option is to cut the hotdogs into bite-sized pieces and completely encase them in the dough, making pretzel nuggets.

Once everything is wrapped—or in batches, if you choose—drop 2 or 3 dough-wrapped hot dogs into boiling water at a time for 30 seconds then using the spider, move them to the baking sheets. Arrange the boiled pretzel items on the prepared baking sheets. Brush each with the egg yolk mixture, and sprinkle with the remaining ¼ cup salt or preferred topping.

Bake in the preheated oven until golden brown, about 15 minutes.

Sausage-Stuffed Mushrooms

INGREDIENTS
16 extra-large white mushrooms
5 tablespoons good olive oil, divided
2½ tablespoons Marsala wine or medium sherry (optional)
½ pounds of loose sweet Italian sausage, or links removed from the casings
4 scallions, white and green parts, minced
2 cloves garlic, minced
½ cup panko crumbs
4 ounces mozzarella cheese
One celery stalk, finely chopped
¼ cup red pepper
¼ cup freshly grated Parmesan
2½ tablespoons minced fresh parsley leaves
Salt and freshly ground black pepper

MATERIALS
Knife
Cutting board
Skillet
Mixing bowl
Measuring spoons and cups

PREPARATION
Preheat the oven to 325F.

Remove the stems from the mushrooms and chop them finely. Set them aside. Place the mushroom caps in a shallow bowl and toss with 3 tablespoons of the olive oil and Marsala. Set them aside.

Heat the remaining 2 tablespoons of olive oil in a medium skillet over medium heat. Add the sausage, crumbling it with the back of a wooden spoon. Cook the sausage for 8 to 10 minutes, stirring frequently, until it's completely browned. Add the chopped mushroom stems and cook for 3 more minutes. Stir in the scallions and garlic and cook for another 2 to 3 minutes, stirring occasionally. Add the panko crumbs, stirring to combine evenly with all the other ingredients. Finally, swirl in the mascarpone and continue cooking until the mascarpone has melted and made the sausage mixture creamy. Off the heat, stir in the Parmesan, parsley, and season with salt and pepper, to taste, Cool slightly.

Fill each mushroom generously with the sausage mixture. Arrange the mushrooms in a baking dish large enough to hold all the mushrooms in a snug single layer. Bake for 50 minutes, until the stuffing is browned and crusty.

Balsamic Marinated Mushrooms Kabob

INGREDIENTS
4 cups mushrooms
2 tablespoons balsamic vinegar
1 tablespoon soy sauce
3 cloves garlic, grated
½ teaspoon thyme
¼ teaspoon salt
¼ teaspoon pepper

MATERIALS
Knife
Cutting board
Skewers
Mixing bowl
Measuring spoons
Grill or baking sheet

PREPARATION

Marinate the mushrooms in the mixture of the remaining ingredients for 30 minutes. Skewer the mushrooms and grill over medium-high heat until just tender and slightly charred, about 2-3 minutes per side

For those not grilling, fifteen minutes in a 550 oven and these are tasty and tender.

Getting Saucy

**Basic Gravy
Smoky Meatloaf Glaze
Meaty Spaghetti Sauce
Throw-Together Sauce**

Basic Gravy

INGREDIENTS
1 cup of meat drippings/broth/reserved liquid
2 tablespoons corn starch
2 tablespoons cold water
1 dash red cooking wine, to taste (optional)

MATERIALS
Saucepan
Small strainer
Small bowl
Measuring spoons and cups

PREPARATION
Combine the cornstarch and water in a small bowl and mix thoroughly, set aside until needed. Pour your meat drippings, broth, or reserved liquid into a small saucepan (strain, if needed). Add the cornstarch mixture and stir until well combined. If desired, add a dash of red cooking wine, to taste. Cook on high until the liquid thickens into a gravy, about two to three minutes, then transfer to a gravy boat and serve on the side with your meal.

Smoky Meatloaf Glaze

INGREDIENTS
1 cup ketchup
2 tablespoons sesame oil
¼ cup honey
2 teaspoons cumin (or to taste)
Dash cayenne pepper (optional)

MATERIALS
Small mixing bowl
Measuring spoons
Mixing spoon
Storage container with an airtight seal

PREPARATION
Combine all ingredients in your bowl and mix well.

SUGGESTIONS
I use this to top my Meat and Veg Loaf recipe (pg. 92), but you could use it anywhere you use barbeque sauce or ketchup.

Meaty Spaghetti Sauce

INGREDIENTS
2 32-ounce cans of crushed tomatoes
1 small onion diced
½ a medium green pepper diced (optional)
½ cup sliced mushrooms (optional)
2 teaspoons minced garlic (fresh or jarred)
1 teaspoon oregano
1 teaspoon sugar
Homemade meatballs (browned, but not cooked)
1 pound sausage, cut into one-inch pieces (browned, but not cooked)
Salt and pepper to taste

MATERIALS
Crockpot
Crockpot liner
Measuring spoons
Mixing spoon
Knife
Can opener
Cutting board

PREPARATION
Combine all ingredients in your crockpot and cook on high for six hours or low for 8 to 10 hours.

THROW-TOGETHER SAUCE

INGREDIENTS
A squirt of olive oil
1 tablespoon butter
1 half an onion, diced
½ cup pine nuts
1 to 2 cloves garlic minced
About 6 or 7 fresh basil leaves chopped
16 ounce can tomato sauce
16 ounce can diced tomatoes (basil and oregano)
1 tablespoon tomato paste
10 kalamata olives
1 teaspoon sugar (optional)

MATERIALS
Knife
Cutting board
Sauté pan
Deep bowl
Stick blender or food processor

PREPARATION
Melt the butter with the olive oil in a sauté pan over medium heat, add pine nuts and onions and sauté until the onions are translucent, stirring constantly so the pine nuts are toasted, but not burnt. Add the garlic and basil, sauté until aromatic, about thirty seconds, before adding the diced tomatoes, sauce, and olives. Simmer to warm. Pour the mixture in to your food processor or a deep bowl if using a stick blender, and pulse until well blended. Return to sauté pan and add tomato sauce. Mix well and heat thoroughly. If the sauce is thicker than you like, add just a touch of water until it is the consistency you desire. If it is too thin, simmer to reduce.

It's Soup Weather

Sausage Soup
Lentil and Ham Soup
**Potato Leek Soup
with Bacon and Cheese**

**Potato Celery Soup
with Sausage and Cheese**

Pot Roast Soup

Sausage Soup

INGREDIENTS
1 pound sweet Italian sausage (loose or in a rope)
1 cup celery, chopped
1 cup carrots, chopped
1 medium onion, diced
1 cup potatoes, diced
½ cup white rice or pasta
4 cups chicken broth
2 cans stewed or diced tomatoes with seasoning (15 ounce)
3 cloves garlic, minced
½ teaspoon of Nature's Seasoning
1 cup water

MATERIALS
Crockpot
Crockpot liner
Measuring spoons and cups
Knife
Cutting board

PREPARATION

Set your crockpot on high for five or six hours, or on low for eight hours.

Process all the produce ingredients and add to the pot with your spices (do not add rice/pasta). Pour in the liquid ingredients. Take your loose sausage meat (or de-case the rope) and either brown the crumpled meat or roll mixture into miniature sausage balls and brown them lightly before adding to the pot. Stir occasionally if desired. Half an hour before cooking time is complete add your rice or pasta as it needs much less time to cook.

Lentil and Ham Soup

INGREDIENTS
1 bag dried lentils, rinsed and sifted
4 cups chicken broth
1 ham bone
1 cup cubed ham
1 cup chopped celery
1 medium onion, diced
1 bay leaf
1 tablespoon garlic
½ teaspoon pepper
2 cups water

MATERIALS
Crockpot
Crockpot liner
Measuring spoons
Knife
Cutting board

PREPARATION
Set your crockpot on high for five or six hours, or on low for eight hours.

Combine all ingredients in a crock pot, stir occasionally, if desired. When cooking time has completed remove all bone fragments and gristle that may result from the use of the ham bone and break up any large pieces of meat that came off the bone. (It is an annoying step, but the use of the bone produces a nice, rich flavor that you won't get from the ham cubes alone.) Thin the mixture with a little water or milk, if needed.

SUGGESTIONS
When on the thick side, the soup also makes a really nice spread or dip, served with or on crackers or bread rounds for an appetizer or finger-food lunch. You can also substitute split peas for the lentils to make this a split pea and ham soup.

Potato Leek Soup with Bacon and Cheddar

INGREDIENTS
2 pounds russet potatoes
3 leeks, whites and greens
½ package of bacon, diced
2 tablespoons minced garlic
3 tablespoons olive oil
1 to 2 cups shredded cheddar, sharp (to taste)
½ to 1 cup of grated parmesan
8 ounces sour cream
6 to 7 cups of chicken broth
¾ cup heavy cream
¼ teaspoon cayenne pepper (optional)
½ cup homemade bacon bits, crispy (optional)
¼ cup sliced scallions, (optional)

MATERIALS
2 Large high-sided bowls
Large soup pot
Measuring spoons
Knife
Mixing spoon
Cutting board
Stick blender or food processor
Two cookie sheets, covered, with sides

PREPARATION
Set your oven to 400F.

Take your potatoes and quarter lengthwise then slice into chunks no more than 1/3 of an inch thick. Place the chunks in a large bowl. Take your leeks and slice into rings roughly ¼ of an inch thick. (I remove any mangled or wilted bits of the dark green but use most of each leek. I find they rinse better if you cut the rings in half. Do not cut the leeks lengthwise before you cut the rings because it makes it harder to cut them.) Add the ring segments to the same bowl as your potatoes. Fill the bowl with water to near the top and swirl the contents of the bowl thoroughly with your hands to separate any sand or grit that might be lodged in the leeks. When you have worked them well remove the cleaned veggies to your second bowl by hand, do not drain or strain as that could redeposit the sand on your cleaned produce. Once you have the potatoes and leeks in the dry bowl add the olive oil, garlic, and bacon to the bowl and mix well. Again, it is best to use your hands as it will give you better control and more even mixture. Once those ingredients are integrated and coated spread them on your cookie sheets. Optimally, you will place both pans in your oven at the same time, either side by side, or one above the other. To ensure even roasting, roast for 20 minutes, take the pans out and turn the mixture, then reverse the placements of the pans in the oven (if it was on the right side, put it on the left; if it was on the top rack put it on the bottom). Roast for another 20 minutes or until tender.

Once the potato/leek mixture has roasted remove any bits that are overly burnt or crispy, then, using either a food processor or a stick blender and bowl, blend into a paste. It's okay to leave some lumps but mix fairly well. Then take your paste and the remaining ingredients (excluding the bacon bits and scallions) and combine in a soup pot on your stovetop, mixing well, simmer on medium until all of the ingredients are well integrated.

Garnish recommendations: crispy bacon bits, scallions, parmesan cheese, or a light sprinkling of cayenne pepper

Variants: Consider adding diced ham, chicken, or steak in the final stage in place of the bacon.

Potato Celery Soup with Crumbled Sausage and Cheese

INGREDIENTS

3 pounds of russet potatoes
5 stalks of celery, diced
½ an onion, diced
½ to 1 pound of loose cooked sausage, crumbled, to taste
2 tablespoons minced garlic
3 tablespoons olive oil
1 cup shredded cheddar, sharp (to taste)
½ cup fresh grated parmesan
8 ounces sour cream
6 to 7 cups chicken broth
¾ cup heavy cream
½ cup cooking sherry
Kosher salt to taste
1 tablespoon fresh rosemary, finely diced
¼ teaspoon black pepper
¼ cup sliced scallions or shallots for garnish (optional)

MATERIALS

Large high-sided bowl
Large soup pot
Measuring spoons
Knife
Mixing spoon
Cutting board
Stick blender or food processor
Two cookie sheets, covered, with sides

PREPARATION

Set your oven to 400F.

Take your potatoes and quarter lengthwise then slice into chunks no more than 1/3 of an inch thick. Place the chunks in a large bowl. Dice your celery and onions and add them to the same bowl as your potatoes. Add the olive oil and garlic to the bowl and mix well. Again, it is best to use your hands as it will give you better control and a more even mixture. Once those ingredients are integrated and coated spread them on your cookie sheets. Optimally, you will place both pans in your oven at the same time, either side by side, or one above the other. To ensure even roasting, roast for 15 minutes, take the pans out and turn the mixture, then reverse the placements of the pans in the oven (if it was on the right side, put it on the left; if it was on the top rack put it on the bottom). Roast for another 15 minutes or until tender.

Once the mixture has roasted remove any bits that are overly burnt or crispy, then, using either a food processor or a stick blender and bowl, blend into a paste. It's okay to leave some lumps but mix fairly well. Then take your paste and the remaining ingredients (excluding your garnishes) and combine in a soup pot on your stovetop, mixing well, simmer on medium until all of the ingredients are well integrated.

Pot Roast Soup

INGREDIENTS
2 tablespoons vegetable oil
Roughly 1 pound of chuck roast
Salt
Pepper
Thyme
1 cup chopped onion (or frozen pearl onions)
1 cup diced carrot
1 cup diced celery
1 can diced potato
1 can diced tomatoes
4 cups beef broth
2 teaspoons beef booster
1 healthy spoonful of jarred mince garlic or fresh cloves, minced, to taste
¼ cup dry barley

MATERIALS
Crockpot
Crockpot liner
Knife
Cutting board
Sauté or frying pan

PREPARATION

Set your Crockpot on high for five or six hours, or on low for eight hours.

If the chuck roast is thin, coat both sides with salt, pepper, and thyme and pat it down so the seasoning sticks. If the chuck roast is thick, cut it in half long-wise and then season as above. Heat the oil in a frying pan or sauté pan. Once the oil is hot, sear the chuck roast three minutes on both sides. Deglaze the pan with a small amount of the beef broth, scraping up the brown bits on the bottom.

Combine the broth from the pan with all the other ingredients except the barley in a lined crockpot. Once the meat is seared, settle that into the crockpot as well. Cook on high for five to six hours, or on low for eight. Half an hour before the soup is done, remove the meat and break it down into small pieces with a spoon, by chopping, or shredding with a fork. (Most likely, it will shred no matter which method you choose.) Return the meat to the pot and add the barley. Stir well and finish cooking. Serve with crusty bread and butter.

(Left: Pot Roast Soup)

That's A Crock

Basic Beef Stew

Apricot-Drenched Country-Style Pork Ribs

SauerApple Pork

Chili – Two Ways

Decadent Pot Roast

Root Beer Pulled Pork

Easy Chicken and Dumplings

Basic Beef Stew

INGREDIENTS
1 pound stew meat
1 cup celery, chopped
1 cup carrots, chopped
1 medium onion, diced
1 cup potatoes, diced
1 32-ounce can crushed tomatoes
2 teaspoons minced garlic, fresh or jarred
½ teaspoon Nature's Seasoning
Flour
Salt and pepper to taste
1 bay leaf (optional)

MATERIALS
Crockpot
Crockpot liner
Measuring spoons and cups
Knife
Cutting board

PREPARATION
Set your crockpot on high for five or six hours, or on low for eight hours.

If the meat is larger than you would like, cut it into smaller pieces. Dredge in flour and brown. (I add the meat raw because it will cook quickly enough and to me the saturation of flavor is better if the meat is not browned first.) Combine all ingredients into the crock pot. Stir occasionally if desired.

SUGGESTIONS
Nice served over egg noodles or white rice, or with crusty Italian bread and butter!

Apricot-Drenched Country-Style Pork Ribs

INGREDIENTS

1 cup apricot brandy
1 large jar apricot sauce (Saucy Susan brand recommended)
Family-sized package of country-style pork ribs (boneless preferred)
2 nice sized cooking apples of choice (Honey Crisp or Cameo are nice)
1 tablespoon chopped garlic (or to taste)
1 large onion (white or yellow) cut in thin slices

MATERIALS

Crockpot
Crockpot liner
Knife
Cutting board
1 to 2 gallon-sized ziplock bags or other sealable container

PREPARATION

8 to 24 hours before cooking place ribs, garlic, and apricot brandy in a ziplock bag or other container, compress to extract as much air as possible while sealing, store in refrigerator to marinade until ready to cook.

Set your Crockpot on high for five or six hours, or on low for eight hours.

Cut onion into slices, cut two apples into thin wedges. Line the bottom of the crockpot with onions in a single layer with maybe a few apple slices mixed in. Hold extras to put on top. Put a layer of rib meat on top of the onions and place apple wedges among them. Coat with Saucy Susan. Put another layer of onions, then another layer of meat and apples. Pour the liquid from the marinade bag over the resulting pile. Coat the top generously with Saucy Susan. Meat should cook down into loose chunks. If you use ribs with the bone in, be sure to sift through the finished dish and extract any bone fragments before serving.

SauerApple Pork

INGREDIENTS
1 to 2 pounds pork chops or 2 to 3 pounds pork roast
1 32-ounce can sauerkraut
1 generous teaspoon of caraway seeds
2 apples, sliced
½ large onion, chopped
½ large onion, sliced (about 4 to 5 slices)
½ cup water

MATERIALS
Crockpot
Crockpot liner
Measuring spoon
Knife
Cutting board

PREPARATION
Set your Crock Pot on high for five or six hours, or on low for eight hours.

Put the sauerkraut with juice into a bowl, add the caraway seeds and mix. Lay onion slices in the bottom of the crock pot, place a layer of pork chops on top of them as-is. Layer with apples and sauerkraut and pork chops until they are all in the pot. Pour sauerkraut mixture over the top of the pork chops and apples. If the sauerkraut isn't enough to cover, add another small can.

Chili Two Ways

With Meat | Vegetarian

INGREDIENTS
- 1 pound meat of choice
- 1 large can of crushed tomatoes
- 1 medium onion, diced
- ½ bell pepper, diced
- 1 can black beans
- 1 can dark red kidney beans
- 1 can small red beans
- 1 tablespoon minced garlic
- Black Pepper
- Paprika
- Chili powder
- Cayenne pepper
- Salt
- Tabasco Sauce

INGREDIENTS
- 1 package veggie burgers
- 1 small eggplant
- 1 large can of crushed tomatoes
- 1 medium onion, diced
- ½ bell pepper, diced
- 1 can black beans
- 1 can dark red kidney beans
- 1 can small red beans
- 1 tablespoon minced garlic
- Black Pepper
- Paprika
- Chili powder
- Cayenne pepper
- Salt
- Tabasco Sauce

MATERIALS
- Crockpot
- Crockpot liner
- Can Opener
- Knife
- Cutting Board

PREPARATION

Set your crockpot on high for five or six hours, or on low for eight hours.

Brown meat and prep all vegetables. Rinse beans, then combine all ingredients into the crockpot, mix well and season to taste.

This recipe is good with the traditional ground beef (or any other ground meat, including sausage); I like to make it with either diced steak or a combination of diced steak and ground beef. Likewise, there are many different types of beans out there are nearly all of them are great in chili. I mix at least three different types for variety in texture and flavor.

GARNISH

Top with either sour cream or shredded cheddar and serve with crusty Italian bread and butter!

PREPARATION

Set your crockpot on high for five or six hours, or on low for eight hours.

Cube veggie burgers and brown, then prep all vegetables. Rinse beans, then combine all ingredients into the crock pot, mix well and season to taste.

There are several different types of veggie burgers that each have a unique texture or flavor. Experiment. Likewise, there are many different types of beans out there are nearly all of them are great in chili. I mix at least three different types for variety in texture and flavor.

GARNISH

Top with either sour cream or shredded cheddar and serve with crusty Italian bread and butter!

Decadent Pot Roast

INGREDIENTS
4 to 5 pounds chuck roast
2 tablespoons canola oil
2 teaspoons Kosher salt
1 teaspoon coarse ground black pepper
1 teaspoon dried thyme
1 pound carrots peeled and cut into 2" chunks
2 pounds small red or Yukon Gold potatoes cut in half
2 cloves garlic minced
2 cups beef broth
1 tablespoon beef booster
2 tablespoons corn starch
2 tablespoons cold water

MATERIALS
Crockpot
Crockpot liner
Frying pan
Knife
Cutting board
Vegetable peeler
Measuring spoons and cups

PREPARATION

Set your crockpot on high for five or six hours, or on low for eight hours.

Season the chuck roast with the Kosher salt, pepper and thyme on both sides.

Heat your pan and add the canola oil. Once the oil is hot, carefully transfer the roast to the pan and brown for 4-5 minutes on each side until you get a nice crust. Deglaze the pan with a small amount of the beef broth, scraping up the brown bits on the bottom. Do not discard, you will add this with the rest of the broth to the crockpot.

In your slow cooker add the carrots, potatoes, and garlic. Lay the beef on top, then add the beef broth and cover.

Once the roast is, combine the cornstarch and water in a small bowl and mix thoroughly. Transfer your roast and the vegetables to a serving platter or container. Pour the liquid from the crockpot through a strainer into a small saucepan and add the cornstarch mixture (I also like to add a dash of red cooking wine). Cook on high until the liquid thickens into a gravy, about two to three minutes, then transfer to a gravy boat and serve on the side with your meal.

Root Beer Pulled Pork

INGREDIENTS
1 Boneless pork shoulder
1 can of root beer
Salt and pepper to taste
Three cloves of garlic, minced

MATERIALS
Crockpot
Crockpot liner
Two forks
Baking sheet or large plate

PREPARATION
Set your crockpot to ten hours.

Rinse and dry your roast, sprinkle with salt and pepper, and add to the crockpot along with the garlic. Pour the root beer over everything and cover.

Remove the pork from the slow cooker onto a sheet tray or large plate. Shred the meat with two forks and discard any large bits of fat. Add the pork back into the slow cooker into the juices. Serve on a bun with of your choice barbeque sauce.

Easy Chicken and Dumplings

INGREDIENTS
1 boneless skinless chicken breast
2 boneless skinless chicken thighs
1 cup chopped yellow onion
1 cup matchstick carrots
1 cup diced celery
4 cloves garlic, minced
1 quart chicken stock
1 tablespoon fresh thyme, or 1 teaspoon dried thyme
2 teaspoons freshly cracked black pepper, or to taste
salt, to taste
2 tablespoons cornstarch
1 12-ounce can evaporated milk

Dumplings:
2 cups all-purpose flour
1 tablespoon plus 1 teaspoon, baking powder
1 teaspoon freshly cracked black pepper
1 teaspoon salt
1 tablespoon fresh thyme, or 1 teaspoon dried thyme
¾ cup whole milk
4 tablespoons butter, melted

MATERIALS
Crockpot
Crockpot liner
Measuring spoons and cups
Mixing bowl
Two forks
Cutting board

PREPARATION
Set your Crock Pot on high for three hours, or on low for seven hours.

Add all of the main ingredients to crockpot except the cornstarch and the evaporated milk.

Right before the time is up, prepare the dough for the dumplings.

In a large bowl, whisk together the dry dumpling ingredients. Make a well in the center of the mixture and pour in the milk and butter. Using a wooden spoon (or rubber spatula), stir together until a dough ball forms. If your mixture seems too dry, add an extra tablespoon of milk. Set aside until ready.

Remove the cooked chicken to a cutting board. Using two forks, shred the meat and return it to crockpot.

Combine the cornstarch and four tablespoons of the evaporated milk in a bowl and mix it until it is smooth to create a slurry. Stir this into the crock pot to thicken the soup then pour in the remainder of the evaporated milk and stir to combine.

Using a spoon, scoop, or even your hands take a bit of the dumpling dough and drop directly into the simmering soup until they form a loose cap over the liquid contents. Do not place them on top of one another or too close. Once all dumplings have been added, gently dunk them under the soup to wet the tops.

If you were cooking on low, change the crockpot to high heat and cook for another hour then check the dumplings for doneness. They may expand and form a seemingly solid mass but should break apart easily at the edges with a little pressure. If they aren't quite finished; cook for another fifteen minutes.

If you do not want the dumplings to absorb too much liquid, when you store the leftovers (if there are any) store the dumplings separate from the main dish.

SIDES HUSTLE

Quick Sauerkraut
Creamy Coleslaw
Asian Pickled Cabbage
Uncle Mike's Sticky White Rice
Uncle Mike's Mashed Potatoes
White Bean Ragout

Quick Sauerkraut

INGREDIENTS
1 cup water
1 cup distilled white or apple cider vinegar
½ onion, diced
1 head cabbage, cored and shredded, but not too thin
¾ teaspoon sea salt
½ teaspoon celery seed
½ teaspoon caraway seed
½ teaspoon onion powder
½ teaspoon garlic powder
ground black pepper to taste

MATERIALS
Knife
Cutting board
Large pot with lid
Measuring cup
Measuring spoons

PREPARATION

Combine all ingredients in the pot. Cover and bring to a boil. Reduce the heat and simmer for three minutes.

Uncover and stir to combine. Cover again and cook, stirring occasionally, until cabbage is tender and wilted, ten to fifteen minutes.

SUGGESTIONS

To make this more of a meal, make the sauerkraut, then fry it in a skillet with butter, a little sugar, and slices of kielbasa.

Creamy Coleslaw

INGREDIENTS
Two cups of cabbage, shredded
One carrot shredded
1 cup mayonnaise
¼ cup sour cream
1½ teaspoons yellow mustard
2 tablespoons apple cider vinegar
3 tablespoons granulated sugar
1 teaspoon celery seeds
1 teaspoon onion powder
¾ teaspoon kosher salt
½ teaspoon black pepper

MATERIALS
Knife
Cutting board
Box grater
Measuring cups and spoons
Silicon spatula

PREPARATION
Place the shredded cabbage and carrots in a large bowl and sprinkle a teaspoon of salt over them.

Toss to combine. Let sit for at least an hour to draw out excess water.

Rinse and drain, then thoroughly dry.

Return the cabbage to the bowl and add the dressing ingredients. Stir until combined. Cover and refrigerate for at least 2 hours before serving.

WHITE BEAN RAGOUT

INGREDIENTS
1 green pepper, diced
2 stalks of celery, diced
½ white onion, diced
3 cloves of garlic, minced
fennel seeds, crushed
Rosemary, minced
2 cans of cannellini or other white beans
1 32-ounce can of diced tomatoes, or two small
Salt
Pepper
Scallions, sliced

MATERIALS
Knife
Cutting board
Skillet

PREPARATION
Combine the ingredients, except the scallions, into a sauté pan and simmer for 20 minutes. Serve over white rice, topped with scallions.

To make this a meal rather than a side, start out by cutting a rope of sausage of your choice into disks and sauteing that in the pan before you add the rest of the ingredients.

Asian Pickled Cabbage

INGREDIENTS
1 small head of cabbage, sliced or chunked
2 carrots shredded, or sliced thin and cut short
¼ cup salt
2 cups water
¾ cup sugar
1 cup white vinegar
3 cloves garlic sliced or smashed
1 inch of ginger, peeled and grated, or sliced very thin
chili peppers, fresh or dried, to taste (optional)

MATERIALS
Large bowl
Plate that will fit inside the bowl
Something heavy to weigh the plate
Cheesecloth or clean kitchen towel
Knife
Cutting board
Micro-plane or grater
Canning jars

PREPARATION
Prepare the cabbage and carrots to your desired size and place in a large bowl. (Note, they will shrink in the process.) Add the salt and mix well with your hands until it is evenly distributed. Place a plate that just fits within the diameter of the bowl on top of the vegetables and weigh it down with something heavy so that the weight and the salt work together to press out as much moisture as possible. Let this marinate for one hour only, refrigerated. If you let it sit longer than that the vegetables will be salty.

While that is marinating, combine the water and the sugar in a small pot and bring it to a boil. Remove it from the heat and stir in the vinegar, along with a half a teaspoon of salt. Cool the liquid completely. Taste for sweet/sour balance and adjust accordingly. Make sure you use a clean spoon or utensil any time you reach into the brine.

Once the hour is up, remove the cabbage and carrots from the refrigerator and wash them thoroughly two to three times to rinse off the salt. Wrap it in a cheesecloth or towel to wring out any excess liquid, then transfer the cabbage and carrots to a clean jar or ceramic container. Add in the rest of the ingredients, including the brine, and mix well. Make sure everything is covered completely.

Store in the refrigerator twenty-four hours before serving. Always use a clean utensil when taking from the jar or the contents will become contaminated and turn.

(No, I don't know how long it lasts. It is never around long enough to tell.)

Uncle Mike's Sticky White Rice

INGREDIENTS
1 cup long grain white rice
2 cups water
1 tablespoon butter or oil
Pinch of salt
Pinch of parsley

MATERIALS
Medium pot
Measuring cup

PREPARATION
Combine ingredients in pot. Bring to a boil. Reduce heat and simmer for fifteen minutes. Remove from heat and let sit for five minutes.

SUGGESTIONS
We serve this with our pot stickers and edamame when we want to make a meal of it, or sesame chicken (pictured here).

Uncle Mike's Mashed Potatoes

INGREDIENTS
6 medium potatoes, peeled and diced
1 clove of garlic, minced
1 stick of butter
1 cup whole milk
Salt to taste

MATERIALS
Large pot
Small sauce pan
Large bowl
Potato peeler
Knife
Colander
Potato masher or electric beater
Cutting board
Measuring spoons and cup

PREPARATION
Fill your large pot with water and add salt, bring to a boil. Add your potatoes and garlic and boil for approximately fifteen minutes, until cooked but still firm. Drain. In a small sauce pan heat the milk and butter until melted. Using your potato masher or electric beater slowly combined your potato, milk, and butter mixtures until smooth and creamy.

The Main Event

Fresh Salsa and Chicken Over Rice

Heart-Stopping, Tummy-Lovin' Mac and Cheese

Garlic-Studded, Rosemary-Crusted Prime Rib

Chicken with Lemon Garlic Rice

Sheppard's Pie

Traditional Cottage Pie

Seared Savory Beef over Rice

Vegetarian Pad Thai

Cheese and Onion Pierogi

Meat and Veg Loaf

Bacon-Wrapped Pork Tenderloin

Fresh Salsa and Chicken Over Rice

INGREDIENTS
2 to 3 pounds boneless chicken
4 to 5 cups minute rice, cooked*
1 quart chicken stock
1 15-ounce can black beans, drained
1 cup flour
Poultry seasoning
Celery salt
Garlic powder
1 cup Traditional Fresh Salsa (pg. 28)
½ cup shredded cheddar

MATERIALS
Casserole pan
Medium bowl or deep plate
Frying pan
Aluminum foil
Non-stick cooking spray

PREPARATION
Preheat oven to 375F.

* Cook minute rice according to the directions on the box, only substitute chicken stock for the required amount of water and add spices to taste. Reserve remaining chicken stock for later in the recipe. Set aside rice to absorb stock.

Rinse chicken thoroughly. Place flour in bowl or deep plate, lightly flour the chicken. Spray frying pan with Pam or lightly spread with olive oil, with pan on medium high, brown chicken (do not cook through). Mix in drained beans with cooked rice and spread in the bottom of the casserole pan until covered. Lay browned chicken across the top of the rice mixture, spread salsa across chicken as evenly as possible (do not cover entire dish). Spread shredded cheddar across all, to taste. Take remainder of the chicken stock from earlier and pour into the casserole. Cover dish with foil and bake for 30 minutes.

Heart-Stopping, Tummy-Lovin' Mac and Cheese

INGREDIENTS
½ pound elbow macaroni (half a box)
1 stick butter
½ cup yellow onion, finely diced
1 clove garlic, minced (or to taste)
3 tablespoons flour
1 tablespoon mustard powder
2 cups heavy cream
½ teaspoon paprika
1 large egg
6 ounces of well-crisped bacon broken into bits, sliced hot dogs, or diced ham
12 ounces sharp cheddar cheese, shredded (or combination of your choice)
1 teaspoon kosher salt
fresh black pepper

Topping
3 tablespoons butter
1 cup panko bread crumbs
Two ounces crispy bacon bits

MATERIALS
Knife
Cutting board
Large pot
Grater
Casserole or aluminum half-pan
Measuring spoons and cups

PREPARATION
Preheat oven to 350F.

Make half a pack of bacon well crisped and break into bits. Reserve two ounces for topping and the rest will be incorporated into the mac and cheese.

In a large pot of boiling, salted water, cook the pasta to al dente.

While the pasta is cooking, in a separate pot, melt the butter. Add in onions and garlic and cook until tender.

Whisk in the flour and mustard and keep it moving for about five minutes making sure it's free of lumps.

Stir in the heavy cream and paprika. Simmer for ten minutes.

Temper in the egg. Stir in ¾ of the cheese and 6 ounces of the bacon or ham. Season with salt and pepper. (if the mixture gets a little too thick/solid add in just a little whole milk until it is creamy again.)

Fold the macaroni into the mix and pour into a 2-quart casserole dish. Top with remaining cheese.

For the topping, melt the butter in a sauté pan and toss the bread crumbs to coat. Top the macaroni with the bread crumbs and bacon bits. Bake for 30 minutes.

Remove from oven and rest for five minutes before serving.

Garlic-Studded, Rosemary-Crusted Prime Rib

INGREDIENTS

(All measures are dependent on the size of your roast.)
Prime rib roast (of any size)
Kosher salt to taste
Black pepper to taste
Fresh rosemary to taste, finely chopped – optional
Garlic cloves, cut into thin slivers, to taste – optional

MATERIALS

Roasting pan to size
Roasting Rack
Knife
Non-stick spray
Aluminum foil
Probe thermometer

PREPARATION

If your roast is fattier than you like, trim the larger portions, but leave some as it imparts moisture and flavor to the finished roast. Generously season all sides of the roast with salt and pepper (but not too much, as you will season again before cooking). Let the roast dry age uncovered in the refrigerator for 24 to 48 hours. The dry aging will cause the seasoning to be drawn into the meat, improving the flavor and making it more tender. The proteins that form on the exterior will give an improved sear. (Optional)

Set your oven to the lowest temperature possible (mine only goes down to 170). Spray your roasting pan or glass baking dish with non-stick spray, then line it with foil. If you have a roasting rack, place it in your dish and spray again with non-stick spray.

If your roast does not come mostly sliced from the bone, cut it now about three quarters of the way the so the bones are still attached, but only just.

Pierce through the roast all over with a narrow-bladed kitchen knife, about every inch or two, across the top and the sides. Slide slivers of garlic into each hole and push them down into the roast, several slivers to each hole. Place a few slivers in the slit between the bones and the roast, as well.

Combine the salt, pepper and rosemary in a bowl then generously season the outside of the roast on all sides, including the slit between the bones and the roast, with the mixture.

Insert a leave-in temperature probe at a 45-degree angle into the thickest part of the roast, being careful not to come in contact with the bones. Set your thermometer to 125 for medium rare or 135 for medium well. How long it roasts will depend on the temperature of your oven and how big the roast is. If your thermometer has a temperature alert use that to gauge when to remove the roast, if not, you will need to monitor the roast to see when the temperature hits your goal.

Once the internal temperature hits the desired goal remove the roast from the oven and remove the temperature probe from the roast. Then set the roast aside to rest for at least half an hour, tenting it with foil to conserve the heat. I place the roast and pan in the microwave so that it is out of the way. If you will not be ready to eat in half an hour, the rest time can go as long as needed, with the next two steps taking place right before you are ready to eat.

As the roast is resting, crank your oven to the highest temperature it will go (mine goes up to 550 degrees). Once the roast is rested, remove the foil tent and return the roast to the oven for ten minutes to sear the exterior.

Remove from the oven. Carve and serve immediately, no need for additional rest time. I first cut off the bone and set aside for later enjoyment, then I hold the roast in place with large tongs and cut the roast into desired slices.

Chicken with Lemon Garlic Rice

INGREDIENTS
1 pound diced chicken (light and dark mixed)
Two cups jasmine rice (dry)
Two cups chicken stock
1 cup water
Juice of half a lemon
¼ tsp pepper
1 clove garlic minced
1 cup frozen peas
Salt and pepper to taste
1 can of cream of chicken soup

MATERIALS
Casserole pan
Medium bowl or deep plate
Frying pan
Aluminum foil
Non-stick cooking spray

PREPARATION
Preheat oven to 350F.

Put chicken stock, peas, water, pepper, lemon, and garlic into a medium saucepan, then add rice. Cook according to the package directions and set aside.

Add chicken to a frying pan and then sprinkle with salt and pepper to taste. Brown chicken, but do not cook it through.

Grease a 9 x 13 pan and fill with rice and peas mixture. Arrange chicken on top. Heat the cream of chicken soup with a little milk to thin it, then pour over the chicken and rice mixture.

Heat for about fifteen to twenty minutes.

Sheppard's Pie

INGREDIENTS
1½ pounds of ground beef
½ cup onion, diced
2 tablespoon minced garlic
1 10-ounce can of vegetable of choice (corn, peas, mixed vegetables)
1 cup of shredded cheese, American or cheddar
1 small jar of tomato sauce or beef gravy, about 1 cup
2 to 3 cups of mashed potatoes (fresh or packaged)
salt and pepper to taste

MATERIALS
Large casserole dish
Large frying pan
Knife
Cutting Board
Spatula
Spoon

PREPARATION
Pre-heat oven to 375F.

In large frying pan, combine meat, spices, garlic, and onion. Sauté until meat is browned. Drain off the fat and move the meat to the casserole dish. Pour in the sauce/gravy and mix well until coated. Spread meat evenly over the bottom of the dish then layer with vegetables.

With your spatula, top the meat-and-vegetable mixture with mashed potatoes to ½ inch below the casserole rim until mixture is completely covered. Do not go to the top of the dish. Spread shredded cheese on top of the mashed potatoes.

Cover casserole with foil and place foil or catch pan beneath in case of bubble-over. Cook about 40 minutes.

POTENTIAL SUBSTITUTIONS
Meat – any ground meat of choice, stew meat, or lamb (if using chunk meat, cut into bite-sized pieces)

For individual portions, follow the above steps, but use single-serving crocks or dishes. Be sure to check the bottoms to confirm they are oven-rated.

Traditional Cottage Pie

INGREDIENTS
2 pounds Yukon gold potatoes, peeled and cut into quarters or to desired size
kosher salt
1 tablespoon olive oil
1 tablespoon butter
1½ pounds lean ground lamb, or meat of your choice
2 teaspoons of kosher salt
1 medium yellow onion, diced
1 cup finely chopped carrots
½ cup fresh peas
4 garlic cloves, peeled and grated
2 teaspoons finely chopped fresh rosemary
black pepper to taste
¼ cup all-purpose flour
1½ cups of water or broth
1 stick of butter at room temperature
6 ounces of cheddar cheese, grated
6 ounces of homemade ricotta cheese (See page 23)
2 tablespoons whole milk
1 egg yolk

MATERIALS
Medium saucepan
Skillet or dutch oven
Large bowl
Fork or potato masher
Vegetable peeler
Knife
Cutting board
Casserole dish
Measuring spoons and cups

PREPARATION
Pre-heat the oven to 425F.

Put the potatoes into a medium saucepan and cover with water. Season generously with salt and gently simmer until tender.

While that is cooking, heat your butter and oil in a skillet or dutch oven over medium-high. Once it is foamy, add the ground meat, breaking it up evenly with your spoon. Season with the kosher salt and cook undisturbed until browned underneath. Reduce heat to medium.

Add the onions and carrots and cook until tender, stirring occasionally. Then add the peas, garlic, rosemary, pepper, and flour and stir to combine.

Stir constantly, cooking until the flour begins to smell nutty. Add your water or broth, scraping up the brown bits from the bottom of the pan. Reduce heat to medium-low and simmer until thickened, about 5 minutes.

While that is cooking, drain the potatoes and move them to a large bowl. Mash the potatoes with the butter and cheese. Season with black pepper and kosher salt. Mix well to combine. Beat the egg yolk with 2 tablespoons milk and add it to your mixture.

Spread half the mashed potatoes into the bottom of the dish and layer that with the meat mixture. Top that with the remaining potatoes. For presentation, you can take a fork and run it gently over the top layer of potatoes, scoring the surface in a crosshatch pattern.

Bake until browned and bubbly, about 15 to 20 minutes.

Seared Savory Beef over Rice

INGREDIENTS
1 pound of well-marbled beef
1 carrot, grated
Garlic cloves (to taste), grated
1 inch of ginger, grated
3 to 5 scallions (depending on size), cut thin on the diagonal
5 marinated mushrooms, sliced
Black pepper to taste
Red pepper flakes to taste
2 to 3 cups cooked white rice
1 tablespoon of corn starch
6 tablespoons of Worcestershire sauce
3 tablespoons of soy sauce
3 tablespoons of sesame oil
Dash of mustard oil (optional)
1 tablespoon of rice vinegar
¼ cup of water
Sesame seeds

MATERIALS
Knife
Cutting board
Skillet
Measuring spoons and cups
Plate
Serving bowl

PREPARATION

Cut your beef into very thin 1-inch slices. Combine the wet ingredients (except for the water) into a medium-sized bowl, add black and red pepper to taste. Add beef slices to the bowl to marinade. Coat all pieces well.

Heat cooking oil in a frying pan on med-high, add your beef slices in a single layer and sear a minute on each side. Remove them to a plate as they are seared and set aside. Add the remains of the marinade to the pan, along with the carrot, ginger, mushrooms, garlic, and half of the scallions. Cook a minute or two to soften. Take your corn starch and combine it with one tablespoon of water, mix until smooth and well combined. Add the mixture to the pan and stir well, then add the rest of the water to the pan. Let the sauce reduce down, then add the meat and the accumulated liquid back into the pan. Mix well until everything is well-coated. Heat through. Serve over white rice garnished with the remaining scallions and a sprinkling of sesame seeds.

Vegetarian Pad Thai

INGREDIENTS
6 ounces uncooked rice noodles
2 tablespoons brown sugar
1 teaspoon ginger, peeled and grated
4 tablespoons reduced-sodium soy sauce
4 teaspoons rice vinegar
The juice of one lime
1 tablespoon sesame oil
2 teaspoons olive oil
3 medium carrots, shredded
1 medium sweet red pepper, cut into thin strips
4 green onions, chopped
3 garlic cloves, minced
5 large eggs, lightly beaten and seasoned
¼ cup chopped fresh cilantro
Chopped peanuts, optional
Lime wedges

MATERIALS
Boiling water
Large bowl
Knife
Cutting board
Wok or large frying pan
Measuring spoons and cups
Tongs

PREPARATION
Put the rice noodles in a heat-safe bowl. Boil four cups of water and pour them over the noodles, stirring to ensure all of the noodles are submerged. Once they are sufficiently softened rinse the noodles two or three times to make sure they are thoroughly rinsed.

In a small bowl or measuring cup combine the brown sugar, ginger, soy sauce, vinegar, lime juice, and sesame oil.

In a large nonstick skillet, heat oil over medium-high heat; stir-fry carrots and pepper until crisp-tender. Add green onions and garlic; cook and stir. Remove from pan.

Reduce heat to medium. Pour eggs into same pan; cook and stir until no liquid egg remains. Stir in carrot mixture, noodles, and sauce mixture; heat thoroughly. Top with cilantro and, if desired, peanuts. Serve with lime wedges.

Cheese and Onion Pierogi

INGREDIENTS

For the Dough:
3½ cups all-purpose flour, or more as needed
1 teaspoon kosher salt
¼ cup vegetable oil
1 cup warm water (130F)
2 tablespoons warm water (130F)

For the Buttered Onions:
½ cup unsalted butter
1 large yellow onion, diced
½ teaspoon kosher salt

For the Filling:
3 medium russet potatoes, peeled and quartered
8 ounces ricotta cheese (see pg. 23)
8 ounces sharp cheddar, shredded
1½ teaspoons kosher salt
1 teaspoon ground black pepper
1 pinch cayenne pepper, or to taste

For Serving:
1 tablespoon unsalted butter, or more as needed
2 tablespoons sour cream, or to taste (Optional)
2 teaspoons snipped fresh chives, or to taste (Optional)

MATERIALS

Mixing bowl
Frying pan
Rolling pin
Large platter
Large saucepan
Kitchen spider
Round cookie cutter
Measuring spoons and cups

PREPARATION

Prepare dough: Combine the flour and the salt in a large bowl, making a well in the center. Pour the vegetable oil and 1 cup plus 2 tablespoons warm water into the well. Stir until a shaggy dough forms, just pulling away from the sides of the bowl.

Use a little flour to clean the dough off the spoon.

Transfer the dough to a lightly floured work surface. Knead until you have a smooth, soft dough. You can add a little more flour if it's too sticky but don't add too much. Shape the dough into a ball and wrap it in plastic. Rest the dough on the counter for 1 hour or in the refrigerator for 3 hours to overnight.

Prepare buttered onions: Melt the butter in a skillet over medium heat. Add the onion and salt and sauté until golden brown, 8 to 10 minutes. Turn off the heat and let mixture cool until needed.

Prepare filling: Place the potatoes into a large pot of well-salted water; bring to a boil. Reduce heat to medium-low and simmer until tender, about 20 minutes. Drain well and mash until smooth. Let cool to room temperature, 10 to 15 minutes.

Place ricotta cheese in a bowl and break it up with a spoon. Add salt, pepper, and cayenne, then add the buttered onions. Be sure to drain off most of the butter so you're adding mostly onions. Mix just until ingredients are evenly combined.

Add the mashed potatoes and mix until thoroughly combined. Set aside while you roll the dough.

On a floured surface, roll out a small portion of the dough at a time, keeping the rest covered by a damp cloth to prevent drying out. The rolled dough should be very thin, no more than 1/8-inch thick, or thinner if possible. Cut 3 ½-inch circles out of the dough, saving the scraps for re-rolling.

Add about 2 tablespoons of the filling to the center of each circle. Moisten the edges with a little water, then fold the dough over the filling and seal the two edges together first in the center, then working from the center to the ends, redistributing the filling as needed as you go. Take care not to trap air inside the dough. You can leave the edge the way it is or make it decorative.

Bring a large pot of salted water to a boil. Add the pierogi in batches and cook for about 2 to 3 minutes.

While the pierogi boil, melt butter in a nonstick skillet over medium heat.

Using the spider, carefully transfer the pierogi from the boiling water directly into the skillet. Cook until golden brown, about 2 minutes per side. Repeat until browned.

SUGGESTIONS

Pairs wonderfully with our Spicy Applesauce (pg. 95) and Quick Sauerkraut (pg. 69), also with a dollop of sour cream.

Meat and Veg Loaf

INGREDIENTS
3 pounds ground chuck
6 ounces garlic-flavored croutons
½ teaspoon ground black pepper
½ teaspoon cayenne pepper
1 teaspoon chili powder
1 teaspoon dried thyme
½ onion, roughly chopped
1 carrot, peeled and broken
2 ribs celery, chopped
8 ounces of mushroom caps, chopped
3 whole cloves garlic, chopped
½ red bell pepper
1½ teaspoon kosher salt
1 egg
Glaze with Smoky Meatloaf Glaze (pg. 47)

MATERIALS
Large mixing bowl
Stick blender or food processor
Knife
Cutting board
Measuring spoons and cups
Probe thermometer
Roasting pan
Parchment paper

PREPARATION
Heat oven to 325F.

In a large bowl, combine the spices and vegetables. Pulse with a stick blender until the mixture is of a fine texture. Combine the vegetable mixture and ground chuck with the bread crumb mixture. Season the meat mixture with the kosher salt. Add the egg and combine thoroughly but avoid squeezing the meat.

Transfer the mixture to a parchment-lined roasting pan and mold the shape of the meatloaf as desired. Insert a temperature probe at a 45-degree angle into the top of the meatloaf until it reaches the middle. Do not touch the bottom of the tray with the probe. Set the thermometer for 155 degrees and cook for fifteen minutes.

Glaze the top of the meatloaf with the Smokey Meatloaf Glaze from page 47 and when the fifteen minutes is, then return the loaf to the oven until it reaches temperature.

Bacon-Wrapped Pork Tenderloin

INGREDIENTS
Spice Rub:
½ teaspoon whole fennel seeds
3 cloves garlic, sliced
1 tablespoon finely sliced sage leaves
2 teaspoons freshly ground black pepper
2 teaspoons chopped rosemary
1 teaspoon kosher salt, or more to taste
1 lemon, zested
1 tablespoon olive oil
1 to 2 pounds boneless pork tenderloin
8 strips bacon

MATERIALS
Mortar and pestle or spice grinder
Knife
Cutting board
Cling wrap
Roasting pan
Probe thermometer
Foil

PREPARATION

Place the fennel seeds in mortar and pestle and crush until fine. Add the garlic, sage, pepper, rosemary, salt, and lemon zest and work into a thick paste, 2 or 3 minutes. Add olive oil and pound until the rub is evenly incorporated.

Trim any silver skin off of your tenderloin, then cut a slit ¾ of the way through the center, leaving 1 inch on each end uncut. Spread 1 tablespoon of the rub inside the slit and close the roast. Spread the remaining rub evenly over the outside. Tuck a small piece of the first bacon strip into the slit, wrap it around the roast, repeating until the surface is covered. Try to keep seams on the bottom.

Wrap the roast in cling wrap and refrigerate for 1 hour, or overnight.

Preheat oven to 450F. Line a rimmed baking sheet with aluminum foil; place roast in the center.

Roast in the preheated oven until a probe thermometer inserted into the center registers 134 degrees F (57 degrees C), about 25 minutes. Let the roast rest until the internal temperature rises to 140 to 145F, about ten minutes.

Slice into medallions and serve.

Aren't You Sweet!

**Spicy Applesauce
Caramel Pecans
Candied Ginger
Homemade Granola
Maple Ginger Candied Bacon
Bread Pudding
Creamy Rice Pudding
White Frosting
Auntie D's Famous Carrot Cake
Dark and Fudgy Chocolate Cake
Berry Sauce**

Spicy Applesauce

INGREDIENTS
4 apples, peeled, cored and chopped
¾ cup water
¼ cup white sugar
1 inch knob of ginger, peeled and grated, or to taste
½ teaspoon ground cinnamon

MATERIALS
Large pot with lid
Knife
Cutting board
Melon baller
Potato masher

PREPARATION
Combine apples, water, sugar, ginger, and cinnamon in a saucepan; cover and cook over medium heat until apples are soft, about 15 to 20 minutes.

Allow apple mixture to cool, then mash with a fork or potato masher until it is the consistency you like, then stir to combine.

SUGGESTIONS
We use Gala apples, but you can use what you like. I recommend that if you use Granny Smiths you combine it with another apple as well or the tartness can be a bit overwhelming.

Sometimes, when I am in the mood for a little more richness, I substitute brown sugar for the white specified in the recipe. We have also combined apple and pineapple or apple and pear for a bit of a different treat.

This pairs very well with our Pierogi and Sauerkraut recipes.

CARAMEL PECANS

INGREDIENTS
2 cups whole pecans
4 tablespoons butter
4 tablespoons brown sugar
2 tablespoons heavy cream

MATERIALS
large frying pan
silicon spatula or similar kitchen tool
large plate
parchment or wax paper
large cookie sheet

PREPARATION
In a large frying pan, melt the butter over medium heat. Add in the pecans and mix until well-coated with butter. Once the pecans are coated add in the brown sugar and heavy cream and mix well. Continue to turn the nuts until the resulting caramel starts to thicken. (I flip the nuts over from the bottom so that the caramel layer pours down over the other nuts.) Keep the nuts moving so that they don't burn. When the caramel is noticeably thickened and most of the liquid has boiled off remove the pan from the heat and pour the nuts on a large plate and spread them out. Allow them to cool a few minutes. As they are cooling cover a large cookie sheet with parchment or wax paper. Once the nuts are cool enough to handle lay them one by one on the cookie tray face up and so they are not touching. Once the pan is full, place it in the refrigerator to cool completely. Enjoy!

For something delightfully different, I like to replace the heavy cream with either eggnog or another cream liquor.

Candied Ginger

INGREDIENTS
Fresh ginger root, peeled and sliced
Water or desired liquid as needed
Sugar, or 1-to-1 sugar substitute of your choice, as needed
Flavoring of choice (optional)

MATERIALS
2- to 4-quart saucepan
Kitchen scale
Silicon spatula
regular teaspoon or vegetable peeler
Sharp knife
cutting board
Mixing bowl, with pour spout, if available
Colander
Platter
Water pitcher
drying rack or dehydrator
non-stick spray

PREPARATION
This is an odd recipe. Amounts are variable depending on how much you want to make and how much the ginger cooks down. For my personal process, it is based much on instinct so it is difficult to quantify. I have done the best I can to create a basic recipe.

PROCESSING THE GINGER
Using the flat of a spoon or a vegetable peeler scrap the skin from the ginger rhizome (root) until you have clean white or cream-colored skin. Rinse the peeled ginger then using a mandolin or knife cut the ginger into slices 1/8th of an inch thick. If the ginger is thick, you can use a knife to cut it into bite-sized pieces.

If you aren't making the ginger right away, your best bet is to process the ginger and put it in plastic containers or freezer-safe ziplock bags and freeze the ginger until you are ready to use it.

If you will be making the ginger in a few days, store it in a plastic storage container, add whatever flavor component you want to try if you intend to infuse the ginger with flavors, and add water or your desired liquid to cover, then store in the refrigerator until you are ready to candy it. Don't wait too long, though. Anything more than a few days and it can get weird.

If you are making it right away, place the processed ginger into your saucepan with water or the desired liquid to cover.

Put the pot of ginger over medium high heat and boil for half an hour.

Drain the ginger into a colander over a bowl, reserving the liquid. Put your saucepan on the kitchen scale and use the tare feature to cancel out the weight. Return the ginger to the pot to weigh the ginger. Use the tare feature again to cancel out the weight of the ginger and the pot together. Add sugar to the pot to equal the weight of the ginger. Return the liquid from the bowl to the pot containing the ginger and the sugar. Bring the mixture back to a boil then lower to medium heat, stirring regularly to prevent the sugar from burning. Watch closely. When the liquid begins to look thick and syrupy, and the ginger starts to look translucent the ginger is ready. If the ginger still looks too fibrous you can add more water to extend the cooking time.

Drain the ginger into the colander over the bowl once more. Be careful: the ginger and sugar mixture are very hot. Keep the remaining syrup, which can be used for a variety of purposes. Transfer the ginger to a large plate and spread it out to cool slightly.

DRYING THE GINGER
If you are using a drying rack spray it with non-stick spray then lay out the slices of ginger in a single layer not touching. Put the tray in an out of the way place and allow the ginger to dry. If you wish, set up a fan to blow on the ginger to aid in the process. This method could take quite some time.

If you are using a dehydrator lay the slices of ginger on your trays (I use the plastic mesh inserts) in a single layer without touching. Once all the ginger is on the trays assemble the machine and turn it on the lowest setting. Check after a few hours to gauge the state of the ginger. If the ginger is dry but sticky, you can dredge it in sugar to coat. If it dries and the exterior forms a hard coat you can leave it as is. Store the finished product in an air-tight container.

FLAVOR-INFUSED GINGER
I don't use any hard-fast rules when adding flavors. Wherever possible I use 100% natural juices or organic products. If I am using a store-bought juice or other liquid, I use it in place of the water when I boil the product. When I use citrus, it is generally the juice of one fruit. Preferably squeezed into the water I store the ginger in if I'm not making the ginger right away, but if not, then direct into the pot at the start of the process. When I use herbs, I use fresh. Spices I will use from a jar. Both get put into disposable spice satchels and they go into the pot for the first boil but are taken out before I add the sugar. If I use an extract, it is 100% pure, not imitation. You will have to experiment with amounts depending on the volume of ginger you are making and your own personal taste.

When using a mandolin, ALWAYS use a protective guard. Don't bother with the "ginger mandolin" you may see at the store. They are difficult and dangerous to use, and blood is not a good flavor pairing with ginger.

Homemade Granola

DRY INGREDIENTS
3 cups rolled oats
½ cups ground flax seed
½ cup coconut flakes
2 cups combined finely chopped almonds, pecans, sesame, and pumpkin seeds

WET INGREDIENTS
¼ cup brown sugar (or substitute an equal measure of ginger simple syrup)
¼ cup maple syrup
¼ cup honey
¼ cup vegetable oil (or oil of choice, such as extra virgin olive oil or coconut oil.)
1 egg white

SEASONING
1½ teaspoons salt
2 teaspoons ground cinnamon (or to taste)
2 teaspoons vanilla extract (or to taste)

FRUITS
1 cup raisins or sweetened dried cranberries
2 ounces candied ginger, finely chopped

MATERIALS
Cutting board
Chopping knife (or food processor)
large mixing bowl
two standard cookie sheets (or one large)
parchment paper or aluminum foil
measuring spoons
measuring cups (both dry measure and wet)

This is granola, there are endless variations of what you can put in so don't feel you have to hold to this ingredients list religiously. I've given you my favorite combination, but don't hesitate to experiment or substitute for items you prefer (my husband likes it when I add half a cup of mini chocolate chips, or you could add a dash of cayenne pepper if you like some spice). When I was researching, I came across a site that advised that the only thing you needed to know to make granola was six parts dry to one part wet. What does that mean? If you have six cups of dry ingredients (your nuts and grains), then make sure you have one cup of wet ingredients (your sweeteners and oils). The fruits aren't counted in that measure as they are added to taste after the cooking process.

PREPARATION

Preheat the oven to 300F.

Line two standard (or one large) baking sheets with parchment or aluminum foil.

Combine the dry ingredients (but not the fruit) in a large bowl. Stir together the seasonings and wet ingredients in a saucepan. (If you need to avoid sodium leave out the salt, but otherwise I highly recommend including it. It really brings out the other flavors.) Bring to a boil over medium heat, then pour over the dry ingredients, and stir to coat. Spread the mixture out evenly on the baking sheets.

Bake in the preheated oven until crispy and toasted, about 45 minutes. Turn the mixture every fifteen minutes. The end mixture should be dry and golden brown. Reduce the time slightly if you prefer your granola not to be toasted, but make sure it isn't still wet. Cool, then stir in the fruit or other add-ins before storing in an airtight container.

This is great as a handy snack by itself or sprinkled over yogurt or ice cream

Maple-Ginger Candied Bacon

INGREDIENTS
12 strips of thick-sliced bacon
1/3 cup Maple ginger simple syrup
1 ounce Maple candied ginger
Finely ground black pepper (optional)
1/3 cup Maple ginger simple syrup

MATERIALS
Two to four cookie sheets of the same size
Metal baker's rack either the same size of your cookie sheet or the size of two cookie sheets side by side
Parchment paper or aluminum foil
Bowl
Basting brush
Micro-plane
Non-stick spray

PREPARATION
Preheat oven to 325F.

Cut bacon into 1- or 2-inch slices and put them in a bowl. If desired, season them with pepper. Using your micro-plane, grate the candied ginger overtop the bacon then coat everything with the simple syrup. Be sure to mix it well so that the ginger is evenly distributed, and everything is well coated with the syrup. Cover a baking sheet with parchment paper or foil. Arrange the bacon in a single layer, then cover with another piece of parchment paper or foil. On top of that, place a second cookie sheet of the same size so that the two sheets are nested. This will flatten the bacon as it cooks.

Put the tray in the center of the oven. Bake for 20 minutes. Check the bacon by lifting the top tray and parchment paper. Remove the trays from the oven but do not turn the oven off. Take one clean cookie sheet (or two, depending on the size of your drying rack) and line it with parchment paper or aluminum foil. Spray the drying rack thoroughly with non-stick spray. If you rack is small enough it will nest with a single cookie sheet with nothing overhanging, place the rack on top of it now. If the rack is large enough that you will need to use two cookie trays beneath it, place the cookie trays in the oven first with the sides touching then close the oven. Transfer the partially cooked bacon from their original cookie trays to the drying rack in a single layer. Using the basting brush coat with more of the simple syrup. Place the cookie sheet with the drying rack on top in the middle of the oven. (Or place the drying rack in the oven on top of the two cookies sheet already there.) Bake in 10-minute increments. Watch closely. The bacon should darken and caramelize. It almost looks burnt when it is

Do NOT turn up the temperature. The bacon will crisp more once it is removed from the oven.

If you are out of maple ginger simple syrup you can supplement this by taking real maple syrup and placing it in a saucepan. Then take a piece of peeled fresh ginger and using your micro-plane grate it into the saucepan. Bring it almost to a boil and then lower it to a simmer. You should start to smell a delicious combination of maple and ginger. If you want you can filter out the pieces of ginger, but personally I would leave them in. They add a nice bit of texture/spice to the bacon. The resulting syrup can be used to baste your bacon.

BREAD PUDDING

INGREDIENTS
2 cups milk
¼ cup butter
2 eggs slightly beaten
6 slices of bread, cut in cubes
½ cup of sugar (I substitute maple syrup or brown sugar instead)
1 teaspoon vanilla extract
1 teaspoon of cinnamon or nutmeg
¼ teaspoon of salt
½ cup of brown or golden raisins (or a mix of both)
Hot water

MATERIALS
A medium sized casserole dish or small square baking pan
A large rectangular baking pan large enough to set the other one inside
Mixing spoon
Medium saucepan
Large mixing bowl
Tea kettle
Measuring cup

PREPARATION
Heat oven to 350F.

In a medium saucepan heat milk and butter over medium heat until butter is melted and milk is hot. In a large bowl, mix eggs, sugar, cinnamon, and salt. Stir in bread and raisins, then add milk and butter. Some prefer the bread to remain in cubes, but I like to mix until the bread breaks up and the end mixture is smooth. Pour the mixture into a small crock or square baking pan. Set the small pan into the large pan and set that in the oven. Once in the oven, fill the large pan to about an inch full of hot water. Bake uncovered 40 to 45 minutes or until a knife inserted one inch from the edge comes out clean.

Creamy Rice Pudding

INGREDIENTS
1 gallon whole milk
1 pound jasmine rice (2½ cups)
1½ cups sugar (I prefer brown sugar, but you can use either)
1 teaspoon vanilla extract or the contents of two vanilla beans
½ a box of brown raisins
1 pinch salt
6 jumbo eggs

MATERIALS
A large, non-stick pot
Mixing spoon
Fork
Small mixing bowl
Measuring cup
Large container with lid

PREPARATION
Combine everything except the eggs in a very large pot and bring to a boil. Stir occasionally. Once it boils lower to a simmer and cover. Let simmer for 18 to 20 minutes or until rice is tender. Watch carefully because it still has a tendency to foam over. In your small mixing bowl, beat the eggs into a froth and slowly add to the mixture two minutes before cooking time is complete. Be sure to mix as you pour so the egg blends instead of just cooking. Pour the finished pudding into several big containers. Or, be sensible and just make a half or quarter batch, reducing the ingredients accordingly. Let cool completely before serving. (I portion out a few single servings in custard cups to facilitate eating sooner.)

Note: I can't tell you how much this makes, but I believe the original is a commercial recipe. The recipe does scale down nicely by either half or thirds.

White Frosting

INGREDIENTS
1 cup milk
¼ cup all-purpose flour
Two sticks of butter, softened
1 cup white sugar
1 teaspoon vanilla extract

MATERIALS
Stand mixer, or large bowl and hand mixer
Spatula
Small sauce pan
Measuring spoons and cups

PREPARATION
Place the milk in a small saucepan. Sift in the flour slowly, stirring constantly as you go to prevent lumps. Cook over medium high heat until boiling. Remove from the heat and set aside to cool. I place the pot in the freezer to speed the process with no adverse effect.

Combine the cooled milk mixture in a stand mixer or bowl with the butter, sugar, and vanilla. Beat for 10 to 12 minutes, scraping the bottom of the bowl occasionally. Keep the frosted cakes refrigerated until half an hour before serving.

Auntie D's Famous Carrot Cake

INGREDIENTS

2 cups white sugar
1¼ cups vegetable oil
4 eggs
2 teaspoons vanilla extract
2 cups all-purpose flour
2 teaspoons baking soda
2 teaspoons baking powder
2 teaspoons ground cinnamon
½ teaspoon salt
3 cups grated carrots
1 cup chopped pecans

MATERIALS

Box grater
Stand mixer, or large bowl and hand mixer
Measuring spoons and cups
Two 9-inch cake pans
Parchment paper or non-stick spray

PREPARATION

Preheat the oven to 350F.

Grease and flour two 9-inch cake pans.

Beat the sugar, oil, eggs, and vanilla together in a stand mixer or a large bowl with an electric mixer until well combined. Mix in flour, baking soda, baking powder, cinnamon, and salt. Stir in carrots. Fold in pecans. Pour into the prepared pans.

Bake in the preheated oven until a toothpick inserted into the center of the cake comes out clean, about 40 minutes. Let cool in the pans for 10 minutes, then turn out onto a wire rack and cool completely.

> **I know, I am strange. I cannot stand cream cheese icing. I think, mostly, because I really do not like powdered sugar. Because of this, I do not use cream cheese icing to frost any of my cakes, even when it is expected. Instead, I invariably make White Frosting but with half of the milk replaced with eggnog. I also garnish it with Caramel Pecans (pg. 96), with eggnog replacing the heavy cream.**

Dark and Fudgy Chocolate Cake

INGREDIENTS
1¾ cups all-purpose flour
¾ cup unsweetened Hershey's Special Dark cocoa powder
1½ teaspoon baking powder
1½ teaspoon baking soda
1 teaspoon salt
2 cups white granulated sugar
2 large eggs
1 cup milk
½ cup vegetable oil
2 teaspoons pure vanilla extract
1 tablespoon instant expresso powder
4 ounces of melted dark chocolate wafers (optional)
1 cup boiling water, divided

MATERIALS
Stand mixer, or large bowl and hand mixer
Measuring spoons and cups
Two 9-inch cake pans
Parchment paper or non-stick spray

PREPARATION
Preheat oven to 350F.

Lightly grease 2x 9-inch round cake pans. Line bottom with parchment paper.

Place flour, cocoa, baking powder, baking soda, and salt into a large bowl. You can sift, if desired, but I used a fork to combine and break up any clumps and it worked well. Use two ounces of boiling water to reconstitute the expresso powder. Add this, with the sugar, eggs, milk, oil and vanilla into a stand mixer or large bowl and combine. Add in the dry ingredients and mix well to combine until lump free, but do not overmix.

Pour the remaining boiling water into the batter, mixing well. Cake batter will be a thin consistency.

Pour batter into cake pans and bake for 30-35 minutes or until a wooden skewer inserted into the center comes out clean.

Let cool for 10 minutes, then turn out onto wire racks to cool completely before frosting. I left the parchment paper on the bottom to prevent sticking.

Berry Sauce

INGREDIENTS
2 cups fresh berries of your choice
¼ cup water
1 cup pineapple or orange juice
The zest from one lime
½ cup white sugar
¼ cup cold water
3 tablespoons cornstarch
½ teaspoon almond extract
⅛ teaspoon ground cinnamon

MATERIALS
Saucepan
a fine sieve
spoon
Measuring cup and spoons
Bowl

PREPARATION

In a saucepan over medium heat, combine the berries (I use a combination of blueberries, raspberries, and blackberries), ¼ cup of water, pineapple juice, and sugar. Stir gently and bring to a boil.

Once the berries are very soft, place the sieve over the bowl and pour the berries and liquids through the sieve. With your spoon, mash the berries against the mesh until all of the juices and pulp go through the sieve, or until you are satisfied. Be sure to scrape the outside of the sieve with a clean spoon (so you don't transfer any seeds by using the one you are mashing the berries with) to clear the mixture clinging to the sieve, scraping it in the bowl. When you are done, you should have mostly seeds in the sieve and clean liquid in the bowl.

Once you are satisfied, pour the juices back into the pot over low heat. Then in a cup or small bowl, mix together the cornstarch and ¼ cup cold water. Gently stir the cornstarch mixture into the juice and simmer gently until thick enough to coat the back of a metal spoon, 3 to 4 minutes. Remove from heat and stir in the almond extract and cinnamon. If the sauce is too thick, add a touch of water until it is the consistency you are looking for.

COOKIES!

Pina Colada Cookies

**Limoncello Coconut
with Candied Ginger Cookies**

**Rum Raisin Cookies
Golden Oatmeal Raisin Cookies
Ginger-Glazed Shortbread
Caramel Pecan Snickerdoodles
Ginger-Coconut Macaroons
Orange-Ginger Florentines
Ginger KICK! Spice Cookies
Lemon Ricotta Cookies**

Pina Colada Cookies

INGREDIENTS
2 sticks butter
2 eggs
½ brown sugar
4 tablespoon Rum of your choice
5 tablespoons of cream of coconut (look for it in the drink mixer aisle in a white squeeze bottle)
1 teaspoon of vanilla extract
½ a bag of flaked coconut
½ cup of candied pineapple finely chopped
1 teaspoon salt
1 teaspoon baking powder
2 cups flour

MATERIALS
Cookie sheet, 10 x 15 or 11 x 17 recommended
Silicon baking pads, parchment paper, or foil
Large bowl or stand mixer
Cooling rack
Spatula
Mixing spoon
Small ice cream scoop

PREPARATION
Pre-heat oven to 375F.

Cream together rum, sugar, butter, vanilla, and cream of coconut. Add eggs and mix. Stir in flour and salt until mixed thoroughly. Add flaked coconut and candied pineapple.

Prepare your cookie sheet with silicon pads, parchment paper, or by wrapping it with foil. Spoon the cookie mixture onto the cookie sheet roughly an inch and a half apart using an ice cream scoop. Neaten scoops for uniform cookies and browning.

Bake for 9 to 11 minutes then move to cooling rack.

Limoncello Coconut with Candied Ginger Cookies

INGREDIENTS
2 sticks butter
2 eggs
½ brown sugar
1 cup of white sugar
4 tablespoons of limoncello liquor
½ a bag of flaked coconut
1 teaspoon of vanilla extract
¼ cup of chopped candied ginger finely diced (optional) (coat with sugar to prevent pieces from sticking together)
1 teaspoon salt
1 teaspoon baking powder
2 cups flour

MATERIALS
Cookie sheet, 10 x 15 or 11 x 17 recommended
Silicon baking pads, parchment paper, or foil
Large bowl or stand mixer
Cooling rack
Spatula
Mixing spoon
Small ice cream scoop

PREPARATION
Pre-heat oven to 375F.

Cream together limoncello liquor, sugar, butter, and vanilla. Add eggs and mix. Stir in flour and salt until mixed thoroughly. Add coconut, and candied ginger.

Prepare your cookie sheet with silicon pads, parchment paper, or by wrapping it with foil. Spoon the cookie mixture onto the cookie sheet roughly an inch and a half apart using an ice cream scoop. Neaten scoops for uniform cookies and browning.

Bake for 9 to 11 minutes then move to cooling rack.

Rum Raisin Cookies

INGREDIENTS
2 sticks butter
2 egg
1½ brown sugar
4 tablespoons rum of your choice (I prefer Myers dark rum)
½ a box of brown raisins pre-soaked in an additional 4 tablespoon of rum
1 teaspoon salt
1 teaspoon baking powder
2 cups flour

MATERIALS
Cookie sheet, 10 x 15 or 11 x 17 recommended
Silicon baking pads, parchment paper, or foil
Large bowl or stand mixer
Cooling rack
Spatula
Mixing spoon
Small ice cream scoop

PREPARATION
Pre-heat oven to 375F.

Cream together rum, sugar, butter, and vanilla. Add eggs and mix. Stir in flour and salt until mixed thoroughly. Add rum-soaked raisins.

Prepare your cookie sheet with silicon pads, parchment paper, or by wrapping it with foil. Spoon the cookie mixture onto the cookie sheet roughly an inch and a half apart using an ice cream scoop. Neaten scoops for uniform cookies and browning.

Bake for 9 to 11 minutes then move to cooling rack.

Golden Oatmeal Raisin Cookies

INGREDIENTS

2 sticks butter
2 eggs
¾ cup brown sugar
½ cup granulated sugar
1 teaspoon vanilla extract
½ teaspoon salt
1 teaspoon baking soda
1½ cups flour
3 cups quick or old-fashioned oats, uncooked
1 cup golden raisins

MATERIALS

Cookie sheet, 10 x 15 or 11 x 17 recommended
Silicon baking pads, parchment paper, or foil
Large mixing bowl or stand mixer
Medium mixing bowl
Cooling rack
Spatula
Mixing spoon
Small ice cream scoop

PREPARATION

Pre-heat oven to 350F.

In your large mixing bowl cream together sugar, butter, and vanilla. Add eggs and mix well. In your medium mixing bowl combine your dry ingredients and mix well. Gradually add your dry ingredients to your wet ingredients and mix thoroughly. Add oats and raisins.

Prepare your cookie sheet with silicon pads, parchment paper, or by wrapping it with foil. Spoon the cookie mixture onto the cookie sheet roughly an inch and a half apart using an ice cream scoop. Neaten scoops for uniform cookies and browning.

Bake for 8 to 10 minutes or until golden brown then move to cooling rack.

Ginger-Glazed Shortbread

INGREDIENTS
3 sticks butter, at room temperature
1 cup sugar
1 teaspoon pure vanilla extract
3½ cups all-purpose flour
¼ teaspoon salt
¼ cup (or more as needed) of ginger simple syrup
or
¼ cup of sugar
¼ of water
One inch of fresh peeled and grated ginger

MATERIALS
Cookie sheet, 10 x 15 or 11 x 17 recommended
Large cowl or stand mixer
Spatula
Rolling pin
Cooling rack
Parchment paper
2-inch cookie cutter
Basting brush
Small saucepan

PREPARATION
Preheat the oven to 350F.

Line your cookie sheets with parchment paper.

In the bowl of an electric mixer fitted with a paddle attachment, mix together the butter and 1 cup of sugar until they are just combined. Add the vanilla. If you want an added ginger kick, you could add grated ginger to the cookie batter itself as well. In a medium bowl, sift together the flour and salt, then add them to the butter-and-sugar mixture. Mix on low speed until the dough starts to come together. Dump onto a surface dusted with flour and shape into a flat disk. Wrap in plastic and chill for 30 minutes.

Roll the dough ½-inch thick and cut with a cookie cutter, re-rolling as needed until all the dough is used. Simple shapes are best (circle, square, heart), those with delicate detail can be difficult to extract the dough without breaking off elements. If you wish, you can glaze them before they bake to create a thin shine across the top, or you can glaze them after as indicated below, which produces a slightly sticky top. Bake for 15 minutes, until the edges begin to brown. Allow them to cool to room temperature.

When the cookies are cool, place them on a baking sheet lined with parchment paper.

While the cookies are baking, prepare your simple syrup. Heat the water and sugar in a small saucepan, add the ginger. Bring to a low boil and cook until the sugar is completely melted, and the flavoring has had a chance to incorporate.

Allow the syrup to cool slightly, then use your basting brush to brush it over the top of the cookies. Air-dry the cookies before storing.

VARIATIONS

Lemon Basil Shortbread – add the zest of one lemon and 5 to 8 finely diced basil leaves to the sugar and butter and mix well before adding the flour. Omit the grated ginger and the ginger simple syrup from the recipe and instead sprinkle the tops of the cookies with white, turbinado, or demerara sugar before baking.

Vanilla Rose Shortbread – In addition to the vanilla extract, add one teaspoon of rose water. Omit the grated ginger and the ginger simple syrup from the recipe and instead sprinkle the tops of the cookies with white, turbinado, or demerara sugar before baking.

Caramel Pecan Snickerdoodles

INGREDIENTS
2 sticks butter, softened
1½ cups sugar
2 large eggs
2¾ cups all-purpose flour
½ cup crushed pecans, the size of a currant or smaller
2 teaspoons cream of tartar
1 teaspoon baking soda
¼ teaspoon fine salt
24 caramels cut in half, or more as needed
2 tablespoons sugar
2 teaspoons ground cinnamon
2 tablespoons crushed pecans, the size of a currant or smaller

MATERIALS
Large bowl or stand mixer
Spatula
Cookie sheets
Parchment paper
Cooling rack

PREPARATION
Preheat the oven to 350F.

Line your cookie sheets with parchment paper.

In a large bowl, combine the butter, 1½ cups sugar and the eggs and mix thoroughly with an electric mixer on medium speed until creamy and well combined, 1 to 2 minutes. Sift together the flour, pecans, cream of tartar, baking soda and salt, and stir into the butter mixture. Place the batter into the refrigerator to chill for at least 1 hour, this will firm the dough and make it easier to roll the balls and embed the caramels.

In a small bowl, stir together the remaining 2 tablespoons sugar with the cinnamon and pecans.

Shape the dough into 1-inch balls. Take half of a caramel and press it into the center, reforming the ball around the caramel, then roll each ball in the pecan-cinnamon-sugar, pressing in slightly to firmly seat the larger pecan pieces. Alternately, you can omit the pecans from the cinnamon-sugar mixture and simply place a pecan or pecan piece on top of the balls before baking, slightly pressed in.

Arrange the dough balls 2 inches apart on ungreased cookie sheets. Bake two sheets at a time until the edges of the cookies are set but the centers are still soft, 13 minutes, rotating the sheets halfway through. Transfer the cookies to wire racks for cooling. Repeat with the remaining dough balls. Store in an airtight container.

Ginger-Coconut Macaroons

INGREDIENTS
¾ cup sweetened condensed milk
¼ teaspoon almond extract
1½ teaspoons vanilla extract
¼ teaspoon fine salt
1 large egg white
3 cups shredded unsweetened coconut
1 ounce chopped candied ginger, or one inch peeled and grated fresh ginger
1 (4 ounce) bar semisweet chocolate, chopped, or to taste (optional)

MATERIALS
Cookie sheet, 10 x 15 or 11 x 17 recommended
Large bowl or stand mixer
Spatula
Cookie sheets
Parchment paper
Cooling rack

PREPARATION
Preheat the oven to 350F.

Line your cookie sheets with parchment paper.

Combine condensed milk, almond extract, vanilla extract, salt, and egg white in a bowl. Whisk until thoroughly combined. Add about 2 1/3 cups shredded coconut. Mix with a spatula until mixture is sticky and holds together. Form into balls using a sorbet scoop.

Roll balls in remaining coconut. Space macaroons evenly onto a silicone-lined baking sheet.

Bake in the preheated oven until golden, about 20 minutes. Let cool to room temperature, at least 20 minutes.

Optional Chocolate Dip

Meanwhile, place ¾ of the chocolate in the top part of a double boiler over simmering water. Stir frequently, scraping down the sides with a rubber spatula to avoid scorching, until chocolate is melted, about 5 minutes. Remove from heat and stir in the rest of the chocolate until it melts.

Dip the base of each cooled macaroon about ⅛ inch into the chocolate. Place cookies, chocolate-side down, on parchment paper. Let chocolate harden completely.

Orange-Ginger Florentines

INGREDIENTS
2 cups blanched slivered almonds and chopped pecans
3 tablespoons all-purpose flour
¼ teaspoon salt
1 orange, zest only
2 ounces of candied ginger, minced
¾ cup brown sugar
2 tablespoons heavy cream
2 tablespoons honey
5 tablespoons unsalted butter, softened
½ teaspoon pure vanilla extract
4 ounces dark chocolate or as needed

MATERIALS
Cookie sheet, 10 x 15 or 11 x 17 recommended
Knife
Cutting board
Saucepan
Large bowl
Spatula
Spoon or scoop
Parchment paper

PREPARATION
Preheat the oven to 350F.

Line two large baking trays with silicone baking mats or parchment paper.

Chop the almonds and pecans until fine, but not pasty.

Combine the nuts, candied ginger, flour, and salt in a large bowl. Set mixture aside.

Add the sugar, cream, honey, zest, and butter to a medium saucepan over medium heat. Stir occasionally until the sugar is dissolved. Once it comes to a rolling boil, let it boil for 1 minute. Turn off the heat and stir in the vanilla.

Pour the sugar mixture into the dry mixture and stir just to combine.

Set aside until the batter is cool enough to handle.

Use a scoop of the desired size to measure out the batter. Roll each into a ball and flatten it slightly. Arrange the flattened batter balls on the prepared baking sheets. They will spread, so be sure to leave sufficient room between them for expansion.

Bake the cookies 1 tray at a time until they're thin and golden brown, about 8 to 10 minutes, turning the tray after 5 minutes.

120 Auntie D's Recipes

Once the cookies are out of the oven, let them cool completely before using a thin metal spatula to remove them.

Continue cooking the batter this way until all the cookies are baked.

When the cookies are cooled, melt the chocolate.

Dip the cookies as desired, either individual cookies halfway, or smear a thin layer of chocolate across the bottom of one cookie and sandwich with another. If you are making decorative shapes, you can get creative with this, dipping just one end, or coating the edges.

Have a silicon sheet or parchment paper handy to set the cookies on to let the chocolate set before serving or storing.

Ginger KICK! Spice Cookies

INGREDIENTS

2½ cups all-purpose flour
1 ounce minced candied ginger
2 teaspoons baking soda
¾ cups butter, softened
½ cup each light brown sugar and dark brown sugar, packed
1 large egg
¼ molasses
1 ½ teaspoons finely grated fresh ginger (peel first)
1 ½ teaspoons ground ginger
1 teaspoon ground cinnamon
½ teaspoon ground cloves
Approx. ½ cup sugar (for rolling)

MATERIALS

Cookie sheet, 10 x 15 or 11 x 17 recommended
Large bowl or stand mixer
Spatula
Cookie sheets
Parchment paper
Cooling rack

PREPARATION

Pre-heat oven to 350F.

Combine the flour, candied ginger, and baking soda in a medium bowl, then set aside.

In an electric mixer, beat the butter until it is smooth and creamy, then add both brown sugars. Beat until creamy once more, then add the egg, molasses, fresh ginger, and the spices. Mix until thoroughly blended. Add half the flour mixture and beat on low to mix. Repeat with the second half of the flour mixture. Use a spatula to scrape the sides and incorporate any components that did not incorporate.

When your dough comes together it should be firm and not too sticky. Take about a tablespoon in your hand and roll it in a ball, then roll that in your bowl of sugar to coat. Place cookies on the tray about 1½ to 2 inches apart.

Bake approximately 15 minutes, or until the surface cracks. Cookies should be firm around the edges, but still soft in the middle.

Note: If you like your spice cookies thin and crisp, use a little less flour, if you like them soft and pillowy, use precise measure. They are delicious either way.

Lemon Ricotta Cookies

INGREDIENTS

2½ cups all-purpose flour
1 teaspoon baking powder
1 teaspoon salt
1 stick unsalted butter, softened
2 cups sugar
2 eggs
15 ounces whole milk ricotta cheese (pg. 23)
3 tablespoons lemon juice
1 lemon, zested
Glaze:
1½ cups powdered sugar
3 tablespoons lemon juice
1 lemon, zested

MATERIALS

Cookie sheet, 10 x 15 or 11 x 17 recommended
Large Bowl or stand mixer
Spatula
Cookie sheets
Parchment paper
Cooling rack

PREPARATION

Preheat the oven to 375F.

Cookies:

In a medium bowl combine the flour, baking powder, and salt. Set it aside.

In a large bowl combine the butter and the sugar. Using an electric mixer beat the butter and sugar until light and fluffy, about 3 minutes. Add the eggs, 1 at a time, beating until incorporated. Add the ricotta cheese, lemon juice, and lemon zest. Beat to combine. Stir in the dry ingredients.

Line 2 baking sheets with parchment paper. Spoon the dough (about 2 tablespoons for each cookie) onto the baking sheets. Bake for 15 minutes, until slightly golden at the edges. Remove from the oven and let the cookies rest on the baking sheet for 20 minutes.

Glaze:

Combine the powdered sugar, lemon juice, and lemon zest in a small bowl and stir until smooth. Spoon about ½-teaspoon onto each cookie and use the back of the spoon to gently spread. Let the glaze harden for about 2 hours. Pack the cookies into a decorative container.

A Bit of Tipple

Homemade Ginger Ale

Apple Bourbon Cocktail with Ginger Syrup

Just Peachy Apple Cider

Rum Kick

Shandygaff

Homemade Ginger Ale (brew method)

INGREDIENTS
4 ounces of ginger simple syrup per 1-liter bottle, or to taste
Warm water
1 packet of dry active champagne yeast
Two tablespoons of sugar

MATERIALS
Funnel
empty 1-liter or 2-liter soda bottles (sanitized)
measuring spoons

PREPARATION
Take a cup of warm water (96 to 110F) and add the yeast and sugar. Stir and cover with a cloth to hold the warmth in, allowing it to 'bloom' for five to fifteen minutes. It should form a visible head, like a beer does.

While the yeast is blooming add the simple syrup to your soda bottle using the funnel, then fill most of the way with room temperature filtered water but leave room for expansion.

Once the yeast is ready add one teaspoon of the mixture to each of your prepared bottles. Cap the bottles and tighten, but not too tight. Store in cool place. Check regularly. When the bottles get tight carefully loosen the cap to vent the building gas. Do this at least once or twice a day for two to three days then refrigerate the bottles. Ready to drink in three to six days.

This won't have an alcohol content, but it will be more potent than commercial ginger ale.

Apple Bourbon Cocktail with Ginger Syrup

INGREDIENTS
1½ ounces bourbon whiskey
4 ounces commercial ginger ale (or homemade apple ginger ale and omit the syrup)
1 tablespoon apple ginger simple syrup (or to taste)
Mint to taste

MATERIALS
Glass
Spoon

PREPARATION
Combine. Enjoy.

Just Peachy Apple Cider

INGREDIENTS
Fresh apple cider
Peach brandy (or the rum of your choice)
Cinnamon stick

MATERIALS
A microwave-safe mug, small sauce pan, or Crock Pot
Spoon of appropriate size

PREPARATION
The quantities for this depend on how many servings you wish to make. If it is just for you, take a microwave-safe mug and fill it three-quarters full of apple cider and then top off with your peach brandy or alcohol of choice, then add in a cinnamon stick and microwave on high for one to two minutes, depending on your microwave and heat preferences.

If you are making this for more than just yourself pour the apple cider into a small saucepan and add the cinnamon stick and heat to your preference, then pour into individual mugs and add the brandy to individual tastes.

If you are making this for a party, an hour or two before your guest arrive pour a half gallon or gallon of apple cider into your crock pot and add one or two cinnamon sticks then set the temperature on high. Just before the party begins add a half a cup to a cup of brandy (per your taste) and switch the crock pot to low or warm if it has that setting. Be sure to warn your guests this is a spiked drink. For a non-alcoholic version substitute peach nectar for the brandy.

Rum Kick

INGREDIENTS
1 pint dark rum of choice (Myers is mine)
5 clementines, halved across the segments, peeled
1 can pineapple chunks
1 small jar maraschino cherries, no stems
1 liter ginger ale
1 liter pineapple juice

MATERIALS
Knife
Cutting board
Large jar or container with air tight seal

PREPARATION
Combine ingredients in a jar or other container with an air-tight seal. Stir and cover. Let it sit overnight. Brace yourself.

> **Why Rum Kick? Because it will hit you much harder than a punch if you're not careful!**

Shandygaff

INGREDIENTS
1 can beer of choice
1 can ginger ale, lemonade, or citrus soda

MATERIALS
A tall glass
A spoon

PREPARATION
Pour one half beer and one-half ginger ale into a glass. Enjoy. Repeat.

SUGGESTION
Keep a spoon or your finger inside the glass when you pour to keep this from foaming over.

About the Author

Danielle Ackley-McPhail was a Quarter Finalist in the Favorite Chef competition in 2023. She is best known for her Ginger KICK! brand of homemade, flavor-infused candied ginger, as well as for her legendary book launches, which she fully caters herself. She is the author of the *Ginger KICK! Cookbook* and has worked both sides of the publishing industry for longer than she cares to admit.

She is also an award-winning author and editor, and crafts and sells original costume horns under the moniker The Hornie Lady Custom Costume Horns.

Danielle lives in New Jersey with husband and fellow writer, Mike McPhail and four extremely spoiled cats.

Our Discerning Connoisseurs

A. Parsons
Andrew Francis
Barbara deBary-Kesner
Beth Rimmels
Carol Gyzander
Chris Hulsey
Christopher J. Burke
Cynthia Murphy
David Lee Summers
Elizabeth Perrotti
Ellen C Montgomery
eSpec Books
Isaac 'Will It Work' Dansicker
Jagi Wright
Janice Campbell
Jennifer L. Pierce
John Idlor
JohnDoe
Judith Waidlich
Katrina N Russell
Kim Hamilton
Kreativ Snail
Librarian
Lorraine J. Anderson
Marli Kennedy
Melanie Drake
Melanie Houselog
Michael Natkin
Rob M. Sutton
Saleh M. Abdullah
Scott J. Dahlgren
Sean Otto
Steven and Scott Sobotta (The Twins)
The Creative Fund by BackerKit
Tina M Noe Good
Tracy Popey
Vicki Hsu
Yoshi Perkoff

www.ingramcontent.com/pod-product-compliance
Lightning Source LLC
Chambersburg PA
CBHW080853060526
44107CB00129B/619